Inhalt

Liebe Schülerin, lieber Schüler,

mit diesem Band „Endspurt zum Abitur" können Sie sich anhand von Originalprüfungsaufgaben intensiv auf das Englischabitur vorbereiten. Das Buch versteht sich als Übungsmaterial für Schüler aller Bundesländer und ist gleichermaßen für Grund- und Leistungskursteilnehmer geeignet.

Trotz unterschiedlicher Aufgabenstellung je nach Bundesland liegt der Hauptakzent bei den Abituraufgaben immer auf der Textarbeit. Ziel dieses Bandes ist das intensive Training anhand von Originalprüfungstexten sowohl zu landeskundlichen Themen, als auch aus dem literarischen Bereich. Dabei möchten wir nicht nur fertige Musterlösungen präsentieren, sondern Ihnen darüber hinaus in kleinen und nachvollziehbaren Schritten den Weg zur Lösung zeigen.

Durch die Vielzahl unterschiedlicher Texte und Aufgaben können sich sowohl starke als auch schwächere Schüler angesprochen fühlen.

Bei der Auswahl der Aufgaben wurden die Vereinbarungen der Konferenz der Kultusminister über einheitliche Anforderungen in der Abiturprüfung berücksichtigt. So geben die verwendeten Aufgaben einen repräsentativen Überblick über die Themengebiete, die für das Englischabitur wichtig sind.

Wir wünschen Ihnen viel Spaß und Erfolg mit diesem Band und alles Gute für Ihre Abiturprüfung!

Verfasserinnen und Verlag

Aufbau des Buches

Dieses Buch besteht aus drei Teilen:

- Teil A stellt Ihnen in gebündelter Form noch einmal die wichtigsten Arbeitstechniken vor, die Sie bereits aus Ihrem Englischunterricht kennen, und die Sie brauchen, um die Abiturprüfung erfolgreich meistern zu können. Außerdem beschreibt er Schritt für Schritt, wie die wichtigsten Aufgabenformen in der Abiturprüfung bearbeitet werden.

Teil A:
wichtige Arbeitstechniken

- Teil B enthält elf Originalprüfungsaufgaben mit einer jeweils ausführlichen Bearbeitung. Hier möchten wir Ihnen jedoch nicht nur eine Musterlösung präsentieren, sondern Sie auch in kleinen und überschaubaren Schritten auf dem Weg dorthin begleiten.

Teil B:
Hinführung zu eigenständigen Lösungen

- In Teil C können Sie zahlreiche Stilmittel und literarische Fachbegriffe nachschlagen. Außerdem finden Sie dort sprachliche Start- und Gliederungshilfen, die Ihnen bei der Strukturierung Ihrer Textproduktion eine wichtige Hilfe sein werden.

Teil C:
Fachbegriffe und Formulierungshilfen

Teil B: Während Teil A und Teil C eher als schnelle Hilfe zum Nachschlagen zu verstehen sind, ist dies der eigentliche Übungsteil, den Sie ganz oder auch nur in Teilen durcharbeiten werden.

Teil B

Sie finden zunächst die Prüfungstexte samt komplettem Aufgabenapparat ohne weitere Erläuterungen. So können Sie sich ein genaues Bild von Aufbau, Umfang und Anforderungen der jeweiligen Aufgabe machen. Im Anschluss daran wird im Abschnitt *Lösungsweg und Lösungsvorschläge* jede Aufgabe detailliert besprochen. Zahlreiche Tipps und Hinweise helfen Ihnen, die einzelnen Teilaufgaben optimal zu bearbeiten. Zum Schluss präsentieren wir Ihnen dann eine Musterlösung bzw. einen Lösungsvorschlag.

Abdruck der Originalaufgaben

Bei den **Fragen zum Text** sind diese Lösungsvorschläge in zwei Teile untergliedert: Eine Stoffsammlung gibt stichpunktartig die wichtigsten Lösungsansätze zur Frage aus dem Text wieder. Auf Umformulierungen wird hier noch weitgehend verzichtet. Dadurch erhalten Sie die Möglichkeit, die vorgegebene mit Ihrer eigenen Stoffsammlung zu vergleichen und anschließend auf dieser Grundlage eine eigenständige Lösung zu erarbeiten. Wenn Sie wollen, können Sie sich dabei an dem darauf folgenden Formulierungsvorschlag orientieren.

Fragen zum Text:
Stoffsammlung
und Formulierungsvorschlag

Fertig ausformulierte Vorschläge erhalten Sie auch für die Einleitung der **freien Textproduktion**. Da der Einleitungsteil meist unabhängig von einer persönlichen Meinung ist, bieten wir hier nur einen Vorschlag an.

Freie Textproduktion:
Formulierungsvorschlag für
die Einleitung

Viele Themenstellungen lassen zwei verschiedene Ergebnisse zu. Wo immer dies der Fall ist, erhalten Sie zwei ausformulierte Schlussvarianten, an denen Sie sich orientieren können.

Zwei Formulierungsvorschläge für den
Schluss

Argumentationshilfen für den Hauptteil der freien Textproduktion

Die freie Textproduktion ist eine sehr individuelle Leistung. Daher werden für den Hauptteil des *comment* keine komplett ausformulierten Lösungen angeboten. Vielmehr wird eine Reihe von Argumenten aufgezählt, aus denen Sie sich diejenigen aussuchen können, die Ihnen selbst am meisten zusagen. Unter Zuhilfenahme der verschiedenen Formulierungshilfen aus Teil C können Sie auf der Grundlage dieser Argumentationshilfen einen überzeugenden Hauptteil erstellen.

Lineare Themen

Bei *linearen Themen* (siehe dazu auch S. 12/13) suchen Sie sich aus den vorgeschlagenen Argumenten diejenigen heraus, die Ihnen persönlich am stichhaltigsten erscheinen.

Obwohl Sie bei der Bearbeitung von Themen, in denen nach Ihrer eigenen Meinung gefragt ist, eine der beiden Seiten stärker gewichten werden, werden hier dennoch Argumente für beide Seiten genannt, damit Ihnen in jedem Fall eine ausreichende Argumentationsgrundlage zur Verfügung steht.

Dialektische Themen

Bei *dialektischen Themen* (vgl. S. 12/13) wiederum wählen Sie zu etwa gleichen Teilen aus den Pro- <u>und</u> Contra-Argumenten aus. Damit Sie nicht in Ihrer Meinungsbildung beeinflusst werden, werden grundsätzlich immer zuerst die Pro-Argumente genannt.

Fußnoten bei freien Übersetzungen

Bei den **Musterübersetzungen** wurde darauf geachtet, sie nicht mit zu vielen erklärenden Anmerkungen auszustatten. Solche finden Sie nur dann, wenn als Musterlösung eine freie Übersetzung angegeben wurde, die stark von der wörtlichen Übersetzung abweicht.

Schrägstriche bei Übersetzungsalternativen

Übersetzungsalternativen wurden durch Schrägstriche gekennzeichnet. Eine komplette Darstellung aller möglichen Alternativen ist unmöglich und wäre auch nicht zweckdienlich.

1. Arbeitstechniken

Informationsentnahme

Um dem Text die gefragten Informationen vollständig entnehmen zu können, haben sich zwei Methoden besonders bewährt: Das Unterstreichen der jeweiligen Information, am besten mit unterschiedlichen Farben für die verschiedenen Fragen, oder das Markieren mit Textmarker. Vermerken Sie unbedingt am Rand, auf welche Frage sich der markierte Textabschnitt bezieht.

Farbiges Unterstreichen oder Markieren

Schlagwörter aus dem Text, die zur Beantwortung der Frage beitragen können, schreiben Sie sich ebenfalls an den Rand oder auf ein gesondertes Konzeptblatt.

Schlagwörter notieren

Texterfassung

Besonders bei der Beantwortung von Fragen zu sehr umfangreichen Texten ist es erforderlich, den Text beim Lesen in größere Sinneinheiten einzuteilen (*skimming*).
Bei der Suche nach ganz bestimmten Informationen empfiehlt es sich, den Text zunächst nach Schlüsselbegriffen zu durchsuchen (*scanning*), anstatt ihn intensiv von vorne bis hinten zu lesen.

skimming und *scanning*

Umgang mit dem Wörterbuch

Das im Abitur zugelassene einsprachige Wörterbuch kann eine große Hilfe sein, aber nur, wenn Sie es effektiv zu nutzen wissen. Deswegen sollten Sie über seinen Aufbau gut informiert sein und Dinge wie die Gliederung der Einträge und die darin verwendeten Abkürzungen beherrschen.

Sich genau mit dem Wörterbuch vertraut machen

Wenn Sie ein Wort nachschlagen, so vergewissern Sie sich, dass Sie aus allen möglichen Wortbedeutungen nicht die erstbeste, sondern die im jeweiligen Kontext am besten passende heraussuchen.

Einträge sorgfältig prüfen

Das Wörterbuch dient nicht nur zum Nachschlagen von Vokabeln, sondern – was für den sprachlichen Ausdruck noch viel wichtiger ist – hilft auch in anderen Belangen, wie zum Beispiel der Grammatik (unregelmäßige Verben etc.), Kollokationen und Idiomatik weiter. So zeigen die Beispielsätze in den einsprachigen Wörterbüchern meist alle wichtigen Möglichkeiten der Verwendung des entsprechenden Wortes im Satzzusammenhang. Man kann nachlesen, ob ein Verb mit Gerund oder Infinitiv konstruiert wird oder welche Präposition auf ein bestimmtes Verb folgt etc.

Verschiedene Anwendungsmöglichkeiten des Wörterbuches

Worterschließungstechniken

Greifen Sie nicht unbedingt gleich zum Wörterbuch, wenn Sie auf unbekannte Vokabeln treffen, da das Nachschlagen Ihnen wertvolle Zeit raubt. Wenn sich ein Wort nicht ohnehin aus dem Kontext ergibt, versuchen Sie zunächst, es mithilfe anderer sprachlicher Kompetenzen zu erschließen.

Wörter erschließen statt nachschlagen

| Präfixe und Suffixe erkennen | Lernen Sie die Bedeutung der wichtigsten Präfixe und Suffixe. Scheinbar unbekannte Wörter lassen sich dadurch manchmal leicht erkennen, z. B. *re-new-able* oder *dis-honour-able* etc. Manche solcher Wörter, die nur durch Hinzufügen von Prä- oder Suffixen gebildet werden, finden Sie außerdem noch nicht einmal im Wörterbuch. |

| Rückgriff auf andere Sprachen | Oft hilft es bei der Erschließung von Wörtern, auf andere Sprachen – auch auf die Muttersprache – zurückzugreifen. Viele scheinbar „schwierige" englische Wörter gehen auf einen lateinischen oder französischen Ursprung zurück, wie z. B. *elaboration* oder *subterranean*. |

Wörter zählen

| Nicht jedes einzelne Wort nachzählen | In vielen Bundesländern werden genaue Wortzahlen angegeben, innerhalb deren Rahmen Sie sich bei der Beantwortung der Fragen zum Text oder der freien Textproduktion bewegen müssen. Anstatt ständig jedes einzelne Wort genau nachzuzählen, reicht es vollkommen, die Wörter in einer Zeile zu zählen und mit der Anzahl der geschriebenen Zeilen zu multiplizieren. |

| Verlangte Wortzahl beachten | Wenn Wortzahlen explizit vorgegeben sind, sollten Sie diesen Rahmen um nicht mehr als 10 % überschreiten, sofern mit Ihrer Lehrkraft nichts anderes vereinbart ist. Mit einer geringeren als der angegebenen Wortzahl jedoch lassen sich die meisten Fragen nicht hinreichend beantworten. |

Zeilenangabe

Sowohl beim Auffinden von Textstellen, die Sie zitieren wollen, als auch bei der Suche nach Stilmitteln im Text ist es sinnvoll, sich die genauen Zeilenangaben bereits auf dem Konzeptblatt zu notieren. Dies erspart Ihnen langes Suchen beim Ausformulieren.

Zeilenangaben auf dem Konzeptblatt notieren

Zeilenangaben in der ausformulierten Antwort werden in runden Klammern angegeben, zum Beispiel (l. 3). Wenn die Information in den Zeilen 5 bis 10 zu finden ist, schreiben Sie (ll. 5–10), während (ll. 8, 10) bedeutet, dass die Information zum Teil in Zeile 8 und zum Teil in Zeile 10 zu finden ist. Zeilenangaben wie (ll. 5 ff.) sind nicht exakt genug.

Regeln zu Zeilenangaben

Zitieren

Da in der gesamten Abituraufgabe Ihre eigenen sprachlichen Fähigkeiten im Mittelpunkt stehen, sollten Sie nicht mehr als unbedingt nötig aus der Angabe zitieren. Notwendig sind Zitate jedoch dann, wenn die Aufgabenstellung sie ausdrücklich verlangt (*Give evidence from the text*) oder auch bei Fragen zu Stilmitteln.

So wenig wie möglich zitieren

Zitate müssen immer sofort als solche erkennbar sein, d. h. sie müssen in Anführungsstrichen stehen (vergessen Sie nicht, dass die Anführungsstriche im Englischen immer oben stehen!) und mit einer exakten Zeilenangabe versehen werden (vgl. Zeilenangabe). Manchmal müssen nur Teilsätze zitiert werden. Diese werden dann mit Hilfe von drei Punkten als solche gekennzeichnet. Um ein Zitat in Ihren Satzbau grammatisch korrekt einzufügen, sind manchmal Auslassungen oder Veränderungen nötig. Änderungen müssen in eckige Klammern gesetzt werden, Auslassungen kennzeichnen Sie durch drei Punkte in eckigen Klammern. Längere Passagen sollten nicht zitiert werden.

Zitate in " "
Zeilenangaben in ( )
Teilsätze mit …
Veränderungen in [ ]
Auslassungen mit […]

2. Hinweise zur Bearbeitung ausgewählter Aufgabenformen

Wichtigste
Aufgabenformen:
• Fragen zum Text
• freie Textproduktion
• Übersetzung

Natürlich sieht die Abituraufgabe in jedem Bundesland etwas anders aus und die Aufgabenformen variieren. In manchen Bundesländern wird beispielsweise Wissen aus dem Bereich der Grammatik, der Idiomatik und des Wortschatzes direkt (d. h. ohne konkreten Bezug zum Text) abgefragt. Fast immer muss auch ein zusammenhängender Text aus dem Englischen ins Deutsche übersetzt werden. Was jedoch in allen Prüfungen verlangt wird, ist die **Bearbeitung einer Textaufgabe**, für die den AbiturientInnen ein längerer Textabschnitt mit verschiedenen Aufgaben vorgelegt wird. Es folgen Fragen zum Inhalt bzw. zu Form, Sprache und Struktur etc. Im Anschluss daran folgt eine Aufgabe zur freien Textproduktion (*comment* bzw. *composition*), die sich thematisch oft mehr oder weniger eng an den vorausgegangenen Text anlehnt. Da die rein sprachlichen Fähigkeiten zur Bearbeitung der Aufgaben vorausgesetzt werden müssen und im Rahmen dieses Buches nicht trainiert werden können, möchten wir Ihnen hier ausschließlich konkrete Tipps zum Umgang mit den drei Aufgabenformen *Fragen zum Text, freie Textproduktion* und *Übersetzung* geben.

a. Fragen zum Text

Text zweimal lesen
1. grober Überblick
2. Detailverständnis

Hier sollen Sie zeigen, ob Sie den Textinhalt richtig verstanden haben und ob Sie ihn auch analysieren können. Deshalb sollten Sie **den Text zweimal lesen**: Beim ersten Mal verschaffen Sie sich einen groben Überblick über den Inhalt, danach lesen Sie ihn ein zweites Mal, um die Details zu verstehen und eventuelle Unklarheiten, was Vokabeln betrifft, zu klären. Halten Sie sich auf keinen Fall zu lange mit dem Nachschlagen im Wörterbuch auf, sondern beschränken Sie sich auf die Vokabeln, die für das Textverständnis tatsächlich unabdingbar sind (vgl. Teil Arbeitstechniken).

Erst alle Fragen lesen

Lesen Sie nun alle Fragen aufmerksam durch, bevor Sie mit der Bearbeitung beginnen, damit Sie nicht Gefahr laufen, eine Antwort an der falschen Stelle zu geben. Wenn Ihnen das passiert, und Sie z. B. die Antwort auf Frage 2 bereits unter 1. geben, wird die betreffende Frage mit null Punkten bewertet, da Sie zeigen sollen, dass Sie gezielte Fragen auch gezielt beantworten können.

Jeder Frage
einen Textabschnitt
zuordnen

Im nächsten Schritt versuchen Sie, jeder Frage einen Textabschnitt zuzuordnen. Meistens (nicht immer!) sind die Fragen in chronologischer Reihenfolge gestellt, d. h. die erste Frage bezieht sich auf den ersten Textabschnitt, die zweite auf den darauf folgenden usw. Normalerweise überlappen sich die Fragen nicht. Fragen, die sich auf den gesamten Text beziehen, also z. B. Fragen nach stilistischen Elementen, kommen in der Regel ganz zuletzt.

Besondere Vorsicht ist bei zwei- oder gar mehrteiligen Fragen geboten. Auch in einem einzigen Satz können zwei Fragen verborgen sein, z. B. *Describe the recent changes on the job market and the consequences of these changes for both men and women.* Stellen Sie sicher, dass Sie keine Teilfrage unbeantwortet lassen und deshalb unnötig Punkte verschenken. Achten Sie auch darauf, Ihre Antwort entsprechend der Fragestellung zu strukturieren, also konkret in diesem Beispiel zunächst die Veränderungen auf dem Arbeitsmarkt zu beschreiben und danach auf die Auswirkungen für die betroffenen Männer und Frauen einzugehen.

Achtung bei mehrteiligen Fragen

Strukturierung der Antwort entsprechend der Fragestellung

Als Stoffsammlung können zumeist die entsprechenden Markierungen im Text dienen, es sei denn, es werden zu komplexe Informationen verlangt. Dann empfiehlt es sich, eine Stoffsammlung auf einem gesonderten Blatt anzulegen. Dies ist unerlässlich bei Fragen, die sich auf den gesamten Text beziehen, vor allem also bei einer Stilanalyse. Bei einer solchen Aufgabe sollten Sie zunächst alle geeigneten Textbeispiele schriftlich festhalten und danach entscheiden, welche Ihnen am geeignetsten erscheinen. In der Regel werden nicht mehr als drei verlangt.

Ggf. schriftliche Fixierung der Stoffsammlung

Wenn Sie alle Antworten klar strukturiert haben, können Sie mit der Ausformulierung beginnen. Jede Antwort sollte mit einer Wiederaufnahme der Frage – ggf. umformuliert – beginnen, sodass man aus Ihrer Antwort zweifelsfrei erschließen kann, wie die Frage lautet, auch ohne sie gelesen zu haben.

Wiederaufnahme der Frage zu Beginn der Ausformulierung

Denken Sie bei der Beantwortung daran, dass die Fragen sich nur auf den vorliegenden Textausschnitt beziehen. Das heißt, Ihr Hintergrundwissen, wie umfangreich es auch immer sein mag, ist hier fehl am Platz. Auch auf weiter gehende Interpretationen sowie auf Ihre persönliche Meinung, sofern nicht ausdrücklich danach gefragt ist, müssen Sie hier verzichten.

Keine Interpretation, keine Stellungnahme, kein Hintergrundwissen

Ein Hauptproblem beim Ausformulieren ist der Anspruch, den Originaltext nicht wörtlich zu übernehmen, sondern den Sachverhalt mithilfe von eigenständigen Formulierungen exakt wiederzugeben. Hierbei helfen Umformulierungen mit **Paraphrasen, Synonymen, Antonymen, Definitionen**, etc. Lassen Sie sich aber nicht dazu verleiten, den Originaltext unter Beibehaltung der Struktur einfach Wort für Wort durch Synonyme zu ersetzen.

Darstellung des Sachverhaltes mithilfe eigenständiger Formulierungen

Manchmal, vor allem bei Fragen nach Stilmitteln oder wenn in der Fragestellung ausdrücklich Textbeispiele verlangt werden, sind wörtliche Zitate unumgänglich. Halten Sie sich hier genau an die Zitierregeln (vgl. S. 8).

Vergessen Sie nicht, dass neben dem Inhalt auch Ihre sprachlichen Fähigkeiten bewertet werden. Achten Sie deswegen neben der korrekten Grammatik und Orthografie vor allem auf eine klare sprachliche Strukturierung Ihrer Antworten. Das erreichen Sie am einfachsten, wenn Sie eine Vielzahl passender Strukturwörter (*discourse markers*) (vgl. Teil C S. 146) beherrschen und einzusetzen wissen.

Sprachliche Strukturierung Ihrer Antwort

Frage und Antwort noch einmal durchlesen	Lesen Sie zuletzt die Frage und Ihre Antwort noch einmal durch, um sicherzustellen, dass Sie nichts Wesentliches übersehen haben, vor allem, wenn es sich um eine mehrteilige Frage handelt.
Ergänzungen durch hochgestellte Ziffern	Sollten Sie dabei feststellen, dass Sie tatsächlich etwas Wichtiges vergessen haben oder dass längere Passagen Ihrer Antwort verändert werden müssen, so verweisen Sie eindeutig – am besten mit hochgestellten Ziffern – auf die Ergänzungen, welche Sie (wenn möglich) direkt unter die Aufgabe schreiben.

b. Freie Textproduktion

Ziel der freien Textproduktion	Im Gegensatz zu den Fragen zum Text, die Objektivität den Textaussagen gegenüber verlangen, wird in der freien Textproduktion (*comment/composition*) von Ihnen verlangt, Ihre eigene Meinung mithilfe von Argumenten und Fakten zu untermauern. Hier sollen Sie zeigen, dass Sie in der Lage sind, stichhaltige Argumente zu finden, sie logisch zu strukturieren und mit ihrer Hilfe zu einem überzeugenden Ergebnis zu kommen.
Zielsetzung eines landeskundlichen Themas	Manchmal wird auch ein landeskundliches Thema für die freie Textproduktion angeboten. Hier ist Ihre eigene Meinung nur am Rande gefragt. Im Mittelpunkt steht vielmehr Ihre Fähigkeit, die für das Thema relevanten Fakten aus Ihrem Wissen auszuwählen und sinnvoll zu strukturieren.
Sorgfältige Themenauswahl	In den meisten Bundesländern werden für die freie Textproduktion zwei oder drei Themen zur Auswahl gestellt. Der oft unterschätzte erste Schritt beim Verfassen des *comment* ist es, sich für eines davon zu entscheiden. Um herauszufinden, zu welchem Thema Ihnen die stichhaltigeren Argumente einfallen, sollten sie zu beiden bzw. wenigstens zu zwei von drei Themen eine stichwortartige Stoffsammlung anfertigen. Verwenden Sie lieber etwas mehr Zeit für die Auswahl als hinterher festzustellen, dass Ihnen ein anderes Thema doch besser gelegen hätte. Landeskundliche Themen sollten Sie nur dann bearbeiten, wenn Sie über gute Kenntnisse auf dem jeweiligen Gebiet verfügen.
Verschiedene Themenstellungen	Sehen Sie sich noch einmal genau die Themenstellung an, bevor sie beginnen, Ihre freie Textproduktion zu strukturieren. Wie bereits erwähnt gibt es im Wesentlichen drei Arten von Themenstellung, die sich im Grad ihrer Komplexität unterscheiden:
Lineare Themen	• Lineare Themen, die lediglich eine Argumentation in eine Richtung verlangen. Solche Themen bestehen oft aus einer einfachen Frage, die mit einem Fragewort beginnt (*Why, How, What …*). • Scheinbar lineare Themen, deren ausführliche Bearbeitung jedoch verlangt, dass wenigstens ein Gegenargument angeführt und anschließend entkräftet wird, was der eigenen Argumentation mehr Stärke und Überzeugungskraft verleiht. Dies ist immer dann der Fall, wenn nach der persönlichen Meinung gefragt wird (*Give your opinion, What do you think about …, What is your opinion? Give reasons for your answer …*).

- Dialektische Themen, deren Bearbeitung eine Beleuchtung des Themas von zwei Seiten verlangt. Zum Schluss sollte man sich für eine der beiden Seiten entscheiden. Die Arbeitsanweisung für solche Themen lautet zumeist *Discuss, What are the pros and cons ...,* oder aber die Themenstellung besteht aus einer einfachen Frage ohne Fragewort. Oft wird das Thema auch mit zwei gegensätzlichen Schlagwörtern gestellt (*Computers – blessing or curse? The Internet – enrichment or danger?*).

Dialektische Themen

Nachdem Sie sich für ein Thema entschieden haben, vervollständigen Sie Ihre Stoffsammlung: Erweitern Sie jedes Ihrer Argumente durch mögliche Konsequenzen und/oder stützen Sie sie durch geeignete Beispiele.

Konsequenzen und Beispiele vervollständigen die Stoffsammlung

Aufgrund der zumeist vorgegebenen Höchstzahl von Wörtern, aus denen der *comment* bestehen sollte, ist es eher unrealistisch, insgesamt mehr als drei starke oder vier schwächere Argumente sprachlich überzeugend darzustellen.

Anzahl der Argumente begrenzen

Bringen Sie anschließend Ihre Argumente in eine sinnvolle Reihenfolge: Beginnen Sie mit den schwächeren Argumenten und bauen Sie ihre Argumentation so auf, dass man eine Steigerung erkennen kann. Bei einem dialektischen Thema (Pro und Contra) beginnt der Hauptteil mit den Argumenten, die <u>nicht</u> Ihre Meinung untermauern.

Anordnung der Argumente

Ein gut strukturierter *comment* besteht immer aus den **klar voneinander abgrenzbaren Teilen** Einleitung, Hauptteil und Schluss. Die Einleitung soll zum Thema hinführen und greift die Themenstellung noch einmal auf, damit man beim Lesen weiß, worüber Sie schreiben, auch ohne den Wortlaut der Themenstellung zu kennen. Der Hauptteil besteht aus Ihrer Argumentation, die schlüssig und strukturiert aufgebaut sein sollte (s. o.), während der Schlussteil die Argumentation abrundet, zu einem Ergebnis kommt und eventuell einen Ausblick gibt.

Einleitung Hauptteil Schluss

Es gibt eine Vielzahl von Möglichkeiten, eine Einleitung so zu gestalten, dass sie das Interesse des Lesers weckt und so zum Thema hinführt. Die wichtigsten dieser Möglichkeiten sind:

- Bezugnahme auf aktuelle Ereignisse oder Situationen
- Bezugnahme auf persönliche Erfahrungen
- Hinweis auf Statistiken, Meinungsumfragen oder wissenschaftliche Studien
- Zitate
- Bezugnahme auf Werke der Literatur

(Sprachliche Hilfsmittel hierfür finden Sie im Teil C.)

Beendet wird der Einleitungsteil mit der Wiederholung des Themas und, wenn die Aufgabenstellung lautet: *Give your opinion*, bereits hier mit einer kurzen Äußerung Ihrer persönlichen Meinung.

Im Schlussteil präsentieren Sie das Ergebnis Ihrer Ausführungen; keinesfalls dürfen Sie an dieser Stelle neue Argumente einführen. Auch hier haben Sie wieder verschiedene Möglichkeiten, das Thema abzurunden:

- Wiederaufnahme bzw. Darlegung Ihrer persönlichen Meinung unter Berücksichtigung der Argumentation
- Lösungsansätze für das in der Themenstellung genannte Problem
- differenzierte Stellungnahme
- Ausblick auf die weitere Entwicklung der in der Themenstellung angeschnittenen Situation

(Hilfsmittel für die sprachliche Gestaltung dieser Punkte finden Sie im Teil C)

Nachdem Sie die Struktur Ihres *comment* in Stichpunkten festgelegt haben, können Sie mit der Ausformulierung beginnen. Aus Zeitgründen ist <u>dringend</u> davon abzuraten, eine Rohfassung zu erstellen; zielführender ist es, die Stoffsammlung für Einleitung, Hauptteil und Schluss relativ ausführlich zu gestalten, um bereits im Voraus ein klares Bild darüber im Kopf zu haben, wie der fertige *comment* aussehen soll.

Auch optisch sollte die Struktur Ihres *comment* klar erkennbar sein: Beginnen Sie für jedes Argument einen eigenen Absatz und rücken Sie die jeweils erste Zeile eines jeden Absatzes ein wenig ein.

Lesen Sie zum Schluss Ihren Aufsatz noch einmal aufmerksam durch und achten Sie hierbei vor allem auf die sprachliche Korrektheit Ihrer Ausführungen, da in der freien Textproduktion mehr Wert auf die Sprache als auf den Inhalt gelegt wird.

c. Übersetzung

Auch wenn die Übersetzung in vielen Bundesländern den letzten Prüfungsteil ausmacht, ist es sehr empfehlenswert, sie noch vor der freien Textproduktion anzufertigen. Sie verlieren nämlich wesentlich mehr Punkte, wenn Sie aus Zeitgründen eine unvollständige Übersetzung abliefern als einen *comment* ohne Schluss. Außerdem ist es vor allem bei der Übersetzung äußerst wichtig, möglichst konzentriert zu arbeiten, was allerdings unter Zeitdruck gegen Ende der Prüfungszeit kaum noch möglich ist.

Übersetzung <u>vor</u> *comment/composition* anfertigen

Lesen Sie sich zu Beginn den gesamten Übersetzungstext aufmerksam durch, damit Sie einen groben Überblick über dessen Inhalt bekommen. Oft ist der Übersetzungstext inhaltlich mit der Textaufgabe verwandt, manchmal ist er sogar ein Teil davon.

1. Aufmerksames Durchlesen

Lesen Sie sich den Text ein zweites Mal durch, schlagen Sie dabei die Vokabeln nach, die Sie nicht kennen und halten Sie deren Übersetzung schriftlich fest. Auch Wörter, deren deutsche Entsprechung Sie zu kennen glauben, die allerdings im vorliegenden Kontext keinen Sinn ergeben, sollten Sie mithilfe des Wörterbuchs abklären; möglicherweise gibt es eine zweite Bedeutung, die Ihnen nicht bekannt ist. Lassen Sie sich jedoch keinesfalls dazu hinreißen, jede kleine Unsicherheit in Ihrem Wortschatz mithilfe des Wörterbuchs ausgleichen zu wollen, da dies zu viel wertvolle Zeit kosten würde. Da die Struktur scheinbar schwieriger Sätze nach Abklärung aller Vokabeln oft leichter wird, ist es nicht ratsam, sich Vokabellücken bis zum Schluss aufzuheben.

2. Nochmaliges Durchlesen und Nachschlagen unbekannter Wörter

Klären Sie anschließend fehlerträchtige grammatische Details wie z. B. die Zeiten der Verben. Hier schleichen sich oft aus Unachtsamkeit Fehler ein. Besonders wichtig sind auch Infinitiv-, Gerund- oder Partizipialkonstruktionen, die aufgrund ihrer fehlenden direkten deutschen Entsprechung und der Vielzahl von Übersetzungsmöglichkeiten ins Deutsche bereits im Vorfeld einer besonderen Übung bedürfen.

Fehlerträchtige grammatische Details beachten

Werden Sie sich zunächst über die eigentliche Bedeutung eines jeden Satzes klar, bevor Sie die Übersetzung schriftlich fixieren. Besonders bei komplexen Satzstrukturen ist es sinnvoll, sich zunächst über den Hauptsatz klar zu werden und sich erst dann mit den Nebensätzen zu beschäftigen.

Vom Hauptsatz zum Nebensatz

Jetzt können Sie mit der Niederschrift Ihrer Übersetzung beginnen. Auch hier ist es aus Zeitgründen nicht ratsam, eine Rohfassung zu erstellen; lassen Sie stattdessen nach jeder geschriebenen Zeile eine Zeile frei, so dass Sie genügend Platz für spätere Korrekturen oder Ergänzungen haben.

Keine Rohfassung Leerzeile nach jeder geschriebenen Zeile

Markieren Sie sich immer genau, welche Textabschnitte Sie bereits übersetzt haben, damit Sie nicht Gefahr laufen, Satzteile oder gar ganze Sätze auszulassen.

Bereits Übersetztes markieren

Umgang mit Lücken	Sollten Sie dennoch einen schwierigen Satz(teil) auslassen müssen, so vermerken Sie das in jedem Fall und lassen Sie ausreichend Platz, damit Sie zum Schluss Fehlendes ergänzen können. Denken Sie daran, dass Lücken <u>immer</u> einen maximalen Punktverlust bedeuten, den Sie als letzten Ausweg unter Umständen durch intelligentes Raten minimieren können.
Keine Alternativlösungen	Entscheiden Sie sich immer für <u>eine</u> einzige Lösung; Alternativen sind nicht zulässig und werden in der Regel auch nicht bewertet oder schlimmstenfalls sogar als Fehler angerechnet. Die Alternativen, die Sie in den Musterlösungen dieses Buches finden, sollen Ihnen lediglich die verschiedenen Übersetzungsmöglichkeiten einer bestimmten Vokabel oder Konstruktion in dem jeweiligen Kontext zeigen.
So wörtlich wie möglich, so frei wie nötig	Grundsätzlich gilt bei Übersetzungen: „so wörtlich wie möglich und doch so frei wie nötig". Haben Sie also den Mut, eine freie Übersetzung zu wählen, wenn eine wörtliche Übersetzung nicht mehr idiomatisch klingt. Zusätze wie „wörtlich: …", mit denen manche SchülerInnen unter Beweis stellen möchten, dass sie die wörtliche Übersetzung erkannt haben, werden in der Bewertung nicht berücksichtigt; stehen Sie also zu Ihren freien Übersetzungen.
Nochmaliges Durchlesen des deutschen Textes	Wie alle Prüfungsteile sollten Sie auch die Übersetzung am Ende noch einmal konzentriert durchlesen und auf Fehler prüfen. Achten Sie dabei besonders auf die korrekte deutsche Grammatik, den Sinn und den Sprachfluss im Deutschen. Eine gute Übersetzung liest sich wie ein deutscher Originaltext. Sollten Sie dabei auf offensichtlichen grammatischen oder sinnentstellenden Unsinn stoßen, müssen Sie die entsprechenden Passagen unbedingt ein weiteres Mal überarbeiten.

Texte zu Literatur

1. Death of a Salesman

1.1. Text und Aufgaben

Perhaps more than any other American play, Death of a Salesman captures the confusions and contradictions at the heart of the American experience – between the past and the present, illusion and reality, idealism and materialism, promise and loss. Without his knowing it, Willy speaks
5 for the mass of Americans whose dreams have not been realized, whose hopes have ended in despair. But it is not merely an American play. It has universal impact in its portrayal of human disintegration under the pressures of modern life, in its lament for a vanished past and its criticism of an inadequate present, in its insistence on understanding and compas-
10 sion. Attention must be paid, Linda tells her sons. If failure and despair are tragic, then Willy Loman is a tragic figure deserving our attention.

It is not so much that Willy Loman is in fact a failure but that he reckons himself one. He comes to the end of his life and looks back over what is to him nothing. He feels he has done nothing, accomplished nothing,
15 achieved nothing. He has always, he admits, felt temporary. By what terms do we reckon a man who does his work, maintains a family, pays off a mortgage, elicits deep emotional response from wife and children a failure? We reckon him a failure only if we judge him by the terms with which Willy judges himself. By material standards, by modern defini-
20 tions of success he is a failure. But surely one of Miller's intentions in this play is to call into question those standards, those definitions. We are not to be as confused as Willy is. We are to understand, as he does not, what is and is not possible in modern life.

And we are to take heart from Biff's development. It does not take his fa-
25 ther's death to make Biff realize his own errors. Before Willy's death Biff is able to see his father as a human being and judge him accordingly. He has finally recovered from his shock at discovering his father was not perfect. He is able to love the man he once loved and pity the man he now is. He can criticize his father without relegating him to some inhuman
30 category.

And he is able to do all that because he has finally begun to look at himself, has finally begun to confront his own petty dishonesties, his own inadequacies as a human being, has finally been able to accept himself for

Zu bearbeitender Text

what and who he is. At this point he no longer needs to blame others, to
35   act as judge, jury and executioner. He has moved beyond blame, beyond
judgement to understanding and acceptance.

Willy Loman is the center of Death of a Salesman but Biff Loman is the
hero, the man who grows and develops and comes out on the side of life,
on the side of reality and honesty and compassion. His is the journey
40   Miller insists we all must make, the journey from innocence to experience, from illusion to reality. Never to make that journey is, as we see in
Willy's case, totally self-destructive. Willy is the object lesson we must
not become, a portrait in confusion and self-delusion and, finally and inevitably, self-destruction. But Biff is what we all must do – the need to see
45   things and people as they are, the commitment to accept what is accept-
able, the absolute necessity of self-knowledge.

568 words   *Barry Gross (1971)*

8 *to vanish:* to disappear • 12 *to reckon:* to consider • 17 *to elicit:* here: to get • 24 *to take heart from:* to be encouraged by • 29 *to relegate:* to put into a lower position

I. Language

1. Vocabulary (ohne Wörterbuch zu bearbeiten)

In the following (items a–g) you are to deal with the underlined words/expressions within the given context.

a) 2: "… contradictions <u>at the heart of</u> …
Explain; you may change the sentence structure.

b) 6: "But it is not <u>merely</u> an American play."
Find a suitable substitute; keep to the sentence structure.

c) 6–7: "It has <u>universal impact</u> in …"
Explain; you may change the sentence structure.

d) 8–9: "of an <u>inadequate</u> present, …"
Explain; you may change the sentence structure.

e) 16: "…, <u>maintains</u> a family, …"
Find a suitable substitute; keep to the sentence structure.

f) 26–27: "He has finally <u>recovered</u> from his shock …"
Explain; you may change the sentence structure.

g) 43–44: "… self-delusion and, finally and <u>inevitably</u>, self-destruction."
Explain; you may change the sentence structure.

h) Find the corresponding **abstract** nouns (not the -ing-forms):
15: admit
32: confront
38: grow
40: insist

2. Grammar and Style (ohne Wörterbuch zu bearbeiten)

a) 4: "<u>Without his knowing it</u>, Willy speaks …"
Explain the –ing-form and replace the underlined phrase by a subordinate clause.

b) 14–15: "He feels he has done nothing, accomplished nothing, achieved nothing."
Describe the stylistic device used in this sentence and explain its function.

c) 35: "He has moved beyond blame, …"
Explain the use of the tense.

d) 42–43: "Willy is the object lesson <u>we must not become</u>, …"
Why can the relative pronoun be left out?

II. Comprehension

Answer the following questions in complete sentences. Keep to the information given in the text, but do not quote.

1. In how far does this play, according to the author, reflect typical traits of life in America and of modern life and its deficiencies in general?

2. Why must Willy Loman consider himself a failure, and how do Gross and Miller judge his performance?

3. The author calls Biff Loman the hero of <u>Death of a Salesman</u>. What reasons does he give for this view, and what lesson are we to learn?

III. Comment
Choose <u>one</u> of the following topics:

1. How do you judge Willy's role as a father?

2. In the course of the play Willy frequently recollects the past, and the action takes place partly in the present and partly in the past. Give one or two examples of these time shifts and explain their function.

IV. Translation

In 1963 Martin Luther King published an impassioned essay called "Why We Can't Wait". The subject was segregation, but even at that early date King understood that his real mission was broader social and economic change. "In that separate culture of poverty in which the half-educated Negro lives, an economic depression rages today," he wrote. The solution for that, King realized, would be very complicated.
Twenty years after his death, millions of Americans, black and white, have given up waiting altogether. The war on poverty – one aim of the civil rights movement – has almost been lost. Worse, the moral energy to continue the battle has been weakened by complacency and an appalling game of finger-pointing. Year after year, the agony of the underclass has been seen as the blacks' problem, the government's problem, but not everyone's. The long road back to commitment will not be easy. Ronald Reagan, who owes his two electoral victories almost exclusively to white voters, was determined to leave the issue alone when he came to office. He will retire with a huge budget deficit, which means that large-scale efforts to improve the condition of the underclass will be difficult for his successors.
196 words   *From Newsweek, March 7, 1988*

10 *complacency:* a feeling of satisfaction with oneself • 10 *appalling:* shocking, disgusting •
10 *finger-pointing:* here: mutual accusations

1.2. Lösungsweg und Lösungsvorschläge

I. Language

In the following you are to deal with the underlined words/expressions within the given context.

Je nachdem, ob das Verändern der Satzstruktur erlaubt ist oder nicht, muss man entweder passende Synonyme finden oder den Satz entsprechend umformulieren.

Paraphrasieren bzw. Synonyme finden

1. Vocabulary

a) 2: "contradictions <u>at the heart of</u> ..."
Explain; you may change the sentence structure.

"contradictions <u>that are central to</u> ..."

b) 6: "But it is not <u>merely</u> an American play."
Find a suitable substitute; keep to the sentence structure.

"But it is not <u>only/just</u> an American play."

c) 6–7: "It has <u>universal impact</u> in ..."
Explain; you may change the sentence structure.

"It is of <u>relevance all over the world</u> ..."

d) 8–9: "... of an <u>inadequate</u> present, ..."
Explain; you may change the sentence structure.

"... of a present <u>which is not as good as it should be</u> ..."

e) 16: "... <u>maintains</u> a family ..."
Find a suitable substitute; keep to the sentence structure.

"... <u>provides for/supports</u> a family ..."

f) 26–27: "He has finally <u>recovered</u> from his shock ..."
Explain; you may change the sentence structure.

"He has finally <u>got over</u> his shock ..."

g) 43–44: "... self-delusion and, finally and <u>inevitably</u>, self-destruction."
Explain; you may change the sentence structure.

"... self-delusion and, finally, self-destruction <u>that cannot be avoided</u>."

h) **Find the corresponding abstract nouns (not the ing-form).**

admit: admission; admittance
confront: confrontation
grow: growth
insist: insistence

Aufgaben zu Sprache
und Stil

2. Grammar and Style

a) **4: "Without his knowing it, Willy speaks …"**
Explain the –ing-form and replace the underlined phrase by a subordinate clause.

The underlined form is a *gerund* used instead of a subordinate clause: "Although he does not know it, Willy speaks …"

**Tipp
siehe S. 140**

Erklärung literarischer
Stilmittel in Teil C

b) **14–15: "He feels he has done nothing, accomplished nothing, achieved nothing."**
Describe the stylistic device used in this sentence and explain its function.

The stylistic device of *repetition* is used together with three verbs whose power increases as the sentence progresses. This brings the sentence to a powerful *climax* and emphasises the fact, that he has *completely* failed.

c) **35: "He has moved beyond blame …"**
Explain the use of the tense.

For interpretations we normally use the *present tenses.* Here the *present perfect* is used because it is the *fact* which is important, not the *time when* the action takes place. Furthermore we can add "*up to now*".

d) **42–43: "Willy is the object lesson we must not become, …"**
Why can the relative pronoun be left out?

The relative pronoun can be left out in a *defining relative clause* when the relative pronoun refers to the object of the main clause.

II. Comprehension

Fragen zum Textverständnis

Answer the following questions in complete sentences. Keep to the information given in the text, but do not quote.

1. In how far does this play, according to the author, reflect typical traits of life in America and of modern life and its deficiencies in general?

Die Antwort finden Sie im ersten Absatz des Textes. Achten Sie hier besonders darauf, dass es um den Text des Autors geht und nicht um Ihr Hintergrundwissen das Stück betreffend!

Meinung <u>des Autors</u> ist gefragt

Antwort im ersten Absatz

Stoffsammlung:
typical traits of life in America:
- The play portrays confusions + contradictions (illusion vs. reality etc.) of American society.
- dreams have not been realized, hopes have ended in despair

typical traits of modern life in general:
- human disintegration under the pressures of modern life
- lament for a vanished past
- criticism of an inadequate present
- insistence on understanding and compassion

Formulierungsvorschlag:
According to the author, the play *Death of a Salesman* reflects life in America because it portrays the manifold contrasts in American society. It highlights, for example those between the Americans' past and their present or between their dreams and their real lives. Furthermore, it shows their unrealized dreams and unfulfilled hopes.

More than that it reflects modern life in general with its loss of humanity. It shows people living in a dissatisfying present dreaming of a "better" past. In addition to that it insists on people's need for sympathy and understanding.

2. Why must Willy Loman consider himself a failure, and how do Gross and Miller judge his performance?

Hier finden Sie die Antwort im zweiten Absatz. Achten Sie darauf, dass die Frage zweigeteilt ist. Im ersten Teil sollen Sie darstellen, warum Loman sich als Versager sehen muss, der zweite Teil gibt die Beurteilung Lomans von Seiten Millers und Gross' wieder.

Zweigeteilte Frage

Antwort im zweiten Absatz

Stoffsammlung:
Why must he consider himself a failure?
- he feels he has done, accomplished and achieved nothing
- measured by material standards and modern definitions of success he is a failure

How do Gross and Miller judge his performance?

- he is a man who does his work, maintains a family, pays off a mortgage, elicits a deep emotional response from his wife and children
- material standards etc. are not important

Formulierungsvorschlag:
Willy Loman must consider himself a failure because, looking back over his life, he realizes that materially-speaking his life has not been a success.
Gross however points out that Willy does fulfil his duties as a husband and provider of a family as he pays the mortgage for his house and cares for his family. According to Gross, Miller wanted to challenge these very standards of a materialistic world.

Zweigeteilte Frage!

Antwort in den letzten drei Abschnitten

3. The author calls Biff Loman the hero of *Death of a Salesman*. What reasons does he give for his view, and what lesson are we to learn?

Auch diese Frage besteht wieder aus zwei Teilen, nämlich:
a) Warum wird Biff als Held bezeichnet?
b) Welche Lehre soll der Leser daraus ziehen?
Die Antworten finden Sie in den letzten drei Abschnitten.

Stoffsammlung:
Reasons: Why is Biff the hero?

- he is the one who grows and develops (e. g. from illusion to reality)
- he gets to see his father in a different light
- he has begun to look at himself and has developed an honest image of himself (self-knowledge)

Which lesson are we to learn?

- we are to take heart from his development
- Biff's journey is the one we all must take
- we have to develop, otherwise we destroy ourselves

Formulierungsvorschlag:
The author calls Biff the hero of *Death of a Salesman* because he is the one who undergoes a positive change during the play. He does not expect his father to be perfect any longer and thus learns to regard and love him as a human being. Furthermore, Biff has changed his attitude towards himself and has developed an honest and more realistic image of himself.
According to Gross, Biff's development should encourage us, the readers, to do as he did. Like Biff, we should make "the journey from (…) illusion to reality." (ll. 34/35) which means that we ought to leave behind our illusions in order to gain access to real life.

Choose <u>one</u> of the following topics.

1. How do you judge Willy's role as a father?

Die Frage inwieweit Willy seiner Rolle als Vater gerecht wird, stellt eines der zentralen Themen des Stücks dar. Darauf können Sie in der Einleitung verweisen.

Formulierungsvorschlag zur Einleitung:
One of the pivotal topics of the drama is the relationship between Willy and his sons, or rather between Willy and Biff. Given the fact that Willy has always wanted the best for his sons but that both Biff and Happy have failed to live a life that would commonly be considered as successful and satisfactory, the question arises whether Willy has lived up to his role as a father or not.

Argumentationshilfen dafür:
• The boys adore him.
• They always look forward to Willy's coming home.
• He loves his boys and is proud of them.

Argumentationshilfen dagegen:
• Not only does he let Biff get away with stealing a football from the locker room, he even encourages him and Happy to steal sand and lumber from a nearby construction site. He also encourages Biff to cheat in exams.
• He loves his children rather for their accomplishments than for their own sake. That's why he favours Biff, who is more athletic than Happy.
• He tries to be a pal rather than a father.
• By instilling the values in his boys that are responsible for his own failure, he contributes to their failures, too.
• Even as Biff has grown up, Willy won't let him go his own way but always tries to push him towards what he understands by "success".

Weil eine Gesamtinterpretation des Dramas immer darauf hinauslaufen wird, dass Willy seiner Vaterrolle <u>nicht</u> gerecht wird, werden bei diesem *comment* keine zwei Alternativen für den Schlussteil gegeben.

Nur ein Schluss möglich

Formulierungsvorschlag für den Schluss:
Taking everything into account one cannot but admit that Willy has not lived up to his role as a father. Even though he may have tried hard to be a good father to Biff and Happy, he often accomplished the opposite of what he had intended. Instead of becoming successful and self-confident men, Willy's younger son turns out to be a liar and a braggart, while the elder one becomes a casual worker who only begins to take full responsibility for his own life the moment he frees himself from his father's influence.

Tipp
siehe S. 12

Lineares Thema mit
ein- oder zweiteiligem
Hauptteil (vgl. Teil A)

2. In the course of the play Willy frequently recollects the past, and the action takes place partly in the present and partly in the past. Give one or two examples of these time shifts and explain their functions.

Formulierungsvorschlag zur Einleitung:

All Willy's flashbacks in the drama are somehow related to and triggered off by some event in the present. Thus a web is being created that allows the reader to establish meaningful connections between Willy's present and his past.

Argumentationshilfen:

First flashback:

- It shows Willy's homecoming in better days.
- It shows that the present problems concerning Willy and the Loman family existed even back in the past (Willy's shortcomings as a father, money problems, Willy contradicts himself).
- The first flashback shows that Willy and young Biff love each other and raises the question as to what has caused the conflict between them. In doing so it serves as part of the exposition and builds up suspense.

Flashback in the restaurant:

- It is triggered off by Biff's failure to get a credit from Bill Oliver.
- It reminds Willy of Biff's flunked maths exam and leads up to the Boston hotel room scene.
- It dissolves the tension that has built up since the first flashback as it explains what has come between Biff and Willy.
- The reader needs this scene to fully understand the conflict between father and son.

Formulierungsvorschlag für den Schluss:

Taken on their own, the series of flashbacks seems like a story in its own right with the Boston scene as its climax. Seen in the context of the play as a whole, however, they deliver the necessary background without which the Loman family's present situation cannot be thoroughly understood.

IV. Translation

1963 veröffentlichte Martin Luther King einen leidenschaftlichen Essay (1) mit dem Titel *"Why We Can't Wait"*, zu Deutsch: „Warum wir nicht warten können". (2) Das Thema war die Rassentrennung, aber selbst/schon zu diesem frühen Zeitpunkt verstand King, dass seine wahre Mission/sein wahrer Auftrag eine umfassendere soziale und wirtschaftliche Veränderung war. „In jener eigenen Kultur der Armut, in der der halb gebildete Neger (3) lebt, wütet heute eine wirtschaftliche Depression", schrieb er. King erkannte/war sich klar darüber, dass die Lösung dafür sehr kompliziert sein würde.

Zwanzig Jahre nach seinem Tod haben Millionen Amerikaner, schwarze wie weiße, es völlig aufgegeben zu warten. Der Krieg gegen die Armut – ein Ziel der Bürgerrechtsbewegung – ist fast verloren. Schlimmer noch, die moralische Energie (um) die Schlacht fortzuführen wurde durch Selbstzufriedenheit und ein erschreckendes/widerwärtiges Spiel gegenseitiger Schuldzuweisung gemindert. Jahr für Jahr wurde die Qual der unteren Gesellschaftsschicht als das Problem der Schwarzen angesehen, als das Problem der Regierung, aber nicht als das von jedermann. Der lange Weg zurück zum Engagement wird nicht einfach sein. Ronald Reagan, der seine zwei Wahlsiege fast ausschließlich weißen Wählern verdankt, war bei seinem Amtsantritt entschlossen, das Problem unberücksichtigt zu lassen. Am Ende seiner Amtszeit (4) wird er ein riesiges Haushaltsdefizit hinterlassen, was bedeutet, dass Anstrengungen im großen Maßstab zur Verbesserung der Situation der unteren Gesellschaftsschichten für seine Nachfolger schwierig sein werden.

(1) Da die Übersetzung „Aufsatz" eher an einen Schulaufsatz denken lässt, bleibt hier am besten der englische Gattungsbegriff „Essay" stehen.

(2) Weil Sie nicht wissen können, ob es von dem genannten Essay eine „offizielle" deutsche Übersetzung gibt und wie deren Titel ist, ist es sinnvoll, den Titel des Essays in beiden Sprachen wiederzugeben.

(3) Auch wenn der Begriff heute abfällig klingt, sollten Sie *negro* mit „Neger" übersetzen, da der Begriff zu der Zeit, aus der Kings Essay stammt, völlig neutral war, sowohl im Deutschen als auch im Englischen.

(4) *to retire* bedeutet normalerweise „sich zurückziehen" bzw. „pensioniert werden"; beides trifft für das Ende der Amtszeit eines amerikanischen Präsidenten nicht zu; das einzige passende Verb wäre „abtreten".

2. The Devil's Own

2.1. Text und Aufgaben

Zu bearbeitender Text   A novel by Christopher Newman

Prologue
North Channel of the Irish Sec off Carnlough
Northern Ireland 7973

On this rare, crystal-clear day, young Frankie McGuire knew the content-
ment that any master of his own universe knows. The breeze-rippled sea
was that same deep, unfathomable blue as Connie Murphy's eyes, and
for the second time in his young life he'd been allowed by his father to
5   take the helm of the family fishing boot. Frankie felt his chest swell and
wished Connie Murphy could see him now. Indeed, he spent the idle
hours of each and every day dreaming of how he would some day own
his own deep-sea fishing boat. He would work these same beloved waters while pretty Connie tended home and hearth. They would live a life
10 together like his father and mother shared. Ah, how young Frankie
McGuire yearned for that day. He would hold his true love's hand all
through the night, and kiss her as often as he wished.

After listening to the weather report, Frankie's da had spun the onboard
radio in search of a news broadcast from Belfast. Frankie already knew
15 plenty about the *troubles*. They had set men like Connie's da and his own
father at odds. And lately, those troubles had intensified. As much as he
loved the infant Jesus and the Virgin, he could not fathom why a family's
place of worship could make all that much difference. Didn't he and Connie share the same bright ginger hair, the same mischievous blue eyes
20 and pale freckled flesh that burned such an angry red in the summer
sun?

"… say clashes escalated between Catholic residents along the Falls Road
and the army after a rubber bullet killed a seven-year-old girl," the an-
nouncer droned. "it was fired by a British soldier to disperse a Catholic
25 protest march, which threatened to escalate toward violence."

"Bollocks!" Frankie's da snarled. "it has escalated to violence now, you
bleeding buggers. Damn you all to the deepest hole in hell."

The fact that it was a seven-year-old girl who had been killed, precisely
the same age as Connie, struck Frankie with a strange unknowing fear.
30 Why, he wondered?

His father read the bewildered look in Frankie's eyes and clapped one of those callused and weather-beaten fisherman's hands on Frankie's shoulder. "Don't ask me why, lad. It's a question I can't answer. They just are what they are."

35 Frankie's eyes had returned to the sea. "What are, Da?" "The big boys rule."

Puzzled, Frankie glanced up at his father once again.

"You pick up a gun," his father explained, "someone gets a bullet."

"I don't think I'll be stopping at the pub for a pint t'night, lad," his da de-
40 clared as they reached the fork in the road. "Your mother will be worried, us bein' late and all. Maybe later, once chores are done. Y' did well t'day, lad. Your father is proud a' you. You'll make a right fine fisherman yet."

They had gotten underway at dawn and Frankie was tired, but still he puffed his chest with pride. His da was a man other men in Carnlough
45 looked up to. Catholic men, at any rate. When he spoke his mind before the peat fire at Feeney's pub, his rumbling voice filled the low-ceilinged room and the other drinkers were respectful. Connie Murphy said once, earlier that summer, that her father and others thought his da was a trou-blemaker, but Frankie could not see how. Connor McGuire was fearless,
50 yes. Frankie had never seen him back down to any man, regardless of size. But not a troublemaker. Nay. Connie's own banker father was a troublemaker, always at the head of the parade of Orangemen on Guy Fawkes Day.

The table looked as though it had been laid for quite some while.
55 Frankie's thirteen-year-old sister, Mary Claire, sat scowling over her lace-work in a corner. "Ma," she bowled out. "Da's here at last."

Frankie's mother, clearly fraught with nerves, darted into the room tying her apron. She bussed the cheek of her husband in passing and ordered Frankie to wash. Once grace was said and Connor McGuire had mashed
60 together equal shares of boiled beef and spuds on his plate, he took a mouthful and surveyed his little family with satisfaction. "Frankie is going to make a right fine fisherman, he will," he announced. "Got an in-stinctive feel for the helm."

"His marks in school are excellent," Frankie's mother countered.

65 "Father Dunleavy tells me he'll recommend him for a place at the semi-nar in another two years' time. We could never afford to give him such a fine education as that, Connor."

It was clear from the expression on Connor McGuire's face what he meant to reply to such a notion, but before he could open his mouth, the

70 door behind him burst open. Connor's terrified son felt his breath catch in his throat as three masked men rushed in, all brandishing weapons. Two of the men took aim at Frankie, his mother, and sister, while the third strode toward the table. A surprised and enraged Connor McGuire began to rise and turn. The move brought him eye-to-eye with the muzzle of an

75 automatic pistol. It was aimed point-blank at his face. And just as suddenly as Frankie's da saw it, the gun jumped with a roar, like a clap of thunder. The back of Connor McGuire's skull came off and for Frankie McGuire, directly in its path, the world turned a hot, sticky red.

(shortened)

The Devil's Own, New York 1997, pp. 1–7

13 *da:* short form for father • 19 *mischievous:* schelmisch • 27 *bugger:* (vulg.) asshole • 52 *Orangemen:* members of a Northern Ireland society of Protestants, named after William of Orange

I. Language/Form

1. Find two examples of imagery in this text and explain their effect on the atmosphere.

2. Change the sentences from lines 39–42 into reported speech.

II. Comprehension
(Use your own words as far as possible.)

1. What are Frankie's dreams about his future?

2. What kind of men are Connie's and Frankie's fathers?

3. How does Frankie's day end?

III. Comment
(Choose one of the following topics.)

1. According to the Oxford Advanced Learner's Dictionary, p. 1326, terrorism is "The use of violence and threats of violence especially for political purposes." Does this definition sufficiently explain this phenomenon in our time? Give your opinion.

2. Violence instead of arguments. Is this today's way of solving problems?

3. A good education – a safe way to a successful future? Give your opinion.

IV. Translation

Translate lines 13–27 (from: "After listening"… up to "hole in hell.").

2.2. Lösungsweg und Lösungsvorschläge

Fragen zu Sprache und Stil

I. Language/Form

1. **Find two examples of imagery in this text and explain their effect on the atmosphere**

Tipp
siehe S. 139

Verschiedene Arten von *imagery*

Belegbeispiele im ganzen Text

Hier ist es Ihnen überlassen, welche Art von *imagery*, also Vergleich, Metapher, Personifizierung etc. Sie auswählen und beschreiben. Suchen Sie auf jeden Fall diejenigen Beispiele aus, die Ihrer Meinung nach die stärkste Wirkung hervorrufen.

Oft ist es gar nicht so einfach, die verschiedenen Arten von Bildhaftigkeit auf Anhieb voneinander abzugrenzen. Falls Sie bei einigen Stilmitteln noch unsicher sind, schlagen Sie zunächst in Teil C.1. nach.

Wir geben Ihnen eine größere als die in der Arbeitsanweisung verlangte Anzahl von zwei Beispielen zur Auswahl.

Stoffsammlung:
- l. 3: "… deep unfathomable blue as C. M.'s eyes …" (simile)
- ll. 46–47: "… his rumbling voice filled the low-ceilinged room …" (metaphor)
- l. 57: "… mother darted into the room …" (metaphor)
- l. 74: "… eye-to-eye …" (personification)
- l. 76–77: "… gun jumped with a roar, like a clap of thunder …" (personification)

Bei solchen Fragen kann es nicht schaden, die gefragten Stilmittel in der Einleitung kurz zu erklären.

Formulierungsvorschlag:

Imagery in general is the use of different images to create a picture in the reader's mind that allows him to visualize situations and thus intensify the reader's perception of what he is reading.

In line 3, for example, the author uses a simile when saying "deep unfathomable blue as C. M.'s eyes …" and thus explicitly compares the sea to Connie's eyes. In doing so, he conveys to the reader a clearly imaginable picture of the colour of both, Connie's eyes and the sea. The fact that they are both unfathomable reflects how mysterious both of them are to Frankie.

The author also uses several metaphors to intensify the reader's view of things, for example in lines 46–47, "… his rumbling voice filled the low-ceilinged room …". By calling the voice of Frankie's father "rumbling", he implicitly compares it to thunder that is strong enough to almost materialize and thus fill a whole room. The same effect is achieved when Frankie's mother "darts" into the room (l. 57) like an arrow.

The strongest image is the personification of the gun that kills Connor McGuire. In line 74 the gun's muzzle becomes an eye staring at McGuire. Later on in lines 76–77 it even jumps and thus creates an even more dangerous and most of all gloomy atmosphere when the reader imagines the gun as a threatening person.

2. Change the sentences from lines 39–42 into reported speech.

Erinnern Sie sich noch an die Regeln zur Zeitenfolge in der indirekten Rede? Steht das einleitende Verb in einer Zeit der Vergangenheit, dann wird aus

Präsens → past tense

past tense → past perfect

present perfect → past perfect

past perfect → past perfect

will-future → would

Außerdem sind natürlich Zeit- und Ortsangaben entsprechend zu ändern. Aus *tonight* wird so beispielsweise *that night*.

Um eine sprachlich ansprechende Lösung zu präsentieren, sollten Sie natürlich darauf achten, möglichst verschiedene Verben für die Einleitung der indirekten Rede zu verwenden (*to declare, to explain, …*).

Einleitungsverben bei der indirekten Rede

Formulierungsvorschlag:

When they reached the fork in the road Frankie's dad declared that he didn't think he would be stopping at the pub for a pint that night. He explained that Frankie's mother would be worried about them being late (and all) and said that maybe later, once all the chores were done (he would go). Finally, he said to Frankie that he had done well that night, that he was proud of him and that he would make a right fine fisherman yet.

II. Comprehension
Use your own words as far as possible.

1. What are Frankie's dreams about his future?

Die Antwort auf diese Frage finden Sie im zweiten Teil des ersten Absatzes.

Stoffsammlung:
- He would some day own his own deep-sea fishing boat and work these same beloved waters.
- Connie would tend home and hearth.
- They would live a life together.
- He would hold her hand all night and kiss her as often as he liked.

Formulierungsvorschlag:
Frankie very often dreams of marrying Connie and of living together with her just as his parents do. He sees himself as a loving and caring husband. In his dreams he longs to have his own boat and to be a deep-sea fisherman like his father, while Connie does the housework.

2. What kind of men are Connie's and Frankie's fathers?

Frankies und Connies Väter werden explizit in ll. 43–53 beschrieben. Darüber hinaus kann man einzelne Charakterzüge von Mr McGuire anhand seines Verhaltens und seiner Worte erschließen.

Stoffsammlung:
Mr McGuire
- is a man other Catholic men look up to
- has a rumbling voice
- is respected by others
- is a man Connie's father and others consider a troublemaker
- is fearless and speaks his mind
- is proud of his son
- is probably involved in the troubles in Northern Ireland (violent death!)

Mr Murphy
- is a banker
- is considered a troublemaker by Frankie
- is always at the head of the Orange parade

Formulierungsvorschlag:
From the way the fisherman McGuire talks to Frankie, it is implied that he is proud of his son. He is a fearless man who says what he thinks and thanks to his impressive voice he is respected by other Catholic men, whereas Protestants, Connie's father among them, consider him a troublemaker. His violent death leads us to assume that he is an important figure during "the Troubles" in Northern Ireland on the Catholic side.

Mr Murphy, a banker, on the other hand, is considered a troublemaker by the Catholics as he seems to be one of the leading Orangemen.

3. How does Frankie's day end?

Ausführliche Beantwortung der Frage

Information aus dem ganzen Text

Natürlich kann diese Frage nicht mit einem einzigen Satz beantwortet werden. Vielmehr sollten Sie in Ihrer Antwort auch die Ausgangssituation berücksichtigen, vor deren Hintergrund sich Mr. McGuires Tod ereignet.

Stoffsammlung:
- satisfying day with his father
- dinner with the whole family
- conversation about his success at school and a possible place at the seminar in two year's time
- door bursts open
- three masked men rush in
- two of them guard Frankie, his mother and sister, the third one kills his father.

Formulierungsvorschlag:
After Frankie's return from a satisfying day at sea with his father, the family has dinner together. While eating, they chat about Frankie's success at school and his mother announces that Frankie might get a chance of attending a Catholic seminary school, a school career the McGuires could never afford on their own. All of a sudden, three masked men enter the room. While two of them threaten Frankie, his mother and sister, the third one shoots off the back of Connor McGuire's head, which lands in Frankie's face.

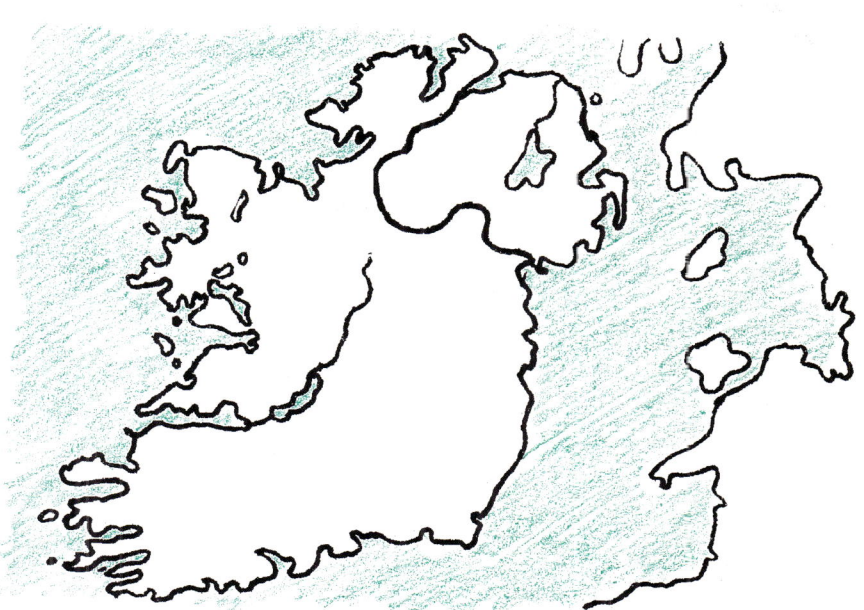

III. Comment

Choose <u>one</u> of the following topics.

1. **According to the** *Oxford Advanced Learner's Dictionary,* **p.1326, terrorism is "The use of violence and threats of violence especially for political purposes." Does this definition sufficiently explain this phenomenon in our time? Give your opinion.**

Argumentation nur in eine Richtung möglich!

Aus logischer Sicht kann die zitierte Definition schon dann nicht mehr ausreichen, wenn auch nur **ein** Aspekt gefunden werden kann, um den die Definition erweitert werden sollte. Da es nicht schwierig sein dürfte, einen solchen Aspekt zu finden, muss die Argumentation zwangsläufig darauf hinauslaufen, dass die zitierte Definition unzureichend ist.

Formulierungsvorschlag zur Einleitung:
Whenever we follow the news on TV or radio, we are confronted with different kinds of terrorist acts all over the world. According to the *Oxford Advanced Learner's Dictionary,* p.1326, terrorism is "The use of violence and threats of violence especially for political purposes." But does this definition sufficiently explain this phenomenon in our time?

Argumentationshilfen:
- The expression "especially for political purposes" leaves too much room for interpretation, because the term "terrorism" is exclusively used in connection with political aims.
- Not all radical political changes that are brought about by violence are necessarily acts of terrorism (e. g. revolutions, wars).
- One important aspect of many terroristic acts that the above definition does not cover is the fact that these acts often affect innocent people who have no involvement whatsoever in the political conflict in question.

Formulierungsvorschlag für den Schluss:
These three arguments contain aspects that can all be taken into consideration to somehow complete the definition given in the OALD. This may be taken as a proof that the definition does not sufficiently explain the phenomenon "terrorism" in our times at all.

2. Violence instead of arguments. Is this today's way of solving problems? Discuss!

Themen wie dieses verleiten oft leicht dazu, eine Bewertung vornehmen zu wollen. Die Themenstellung verlangt jedoch eine Analyse des Ist-Zustandes, nicht des Soll-Zustandes.

Tipp
siehe S. 13

Dialektisches Thema

Keine Bewertung der Situation!

Formulierungsvorschlag zur Einleitung:
Nowadays we almost consider it normal to open our newspaper and find new articles about the latest eruptions of violence everywhere. Following these news stories day by day, it seems as if violence were today's way of solving problems. Is this really true, however?

Argumentationshilfen dafür:
- The number of cases where crazed gunmen are no longer able to deal with their problems verbally and try to give vent to their frustration or to demonstrate their power by randomly threatening or even killing is increasing (e. g. pupils running amok at schools).
- Especially young people with poor prospects for the future tend to deal with their problems by means of violence (e. g. attacks on minorities).
- Even in world politics it can be observed that certain conflicting parties never seem to be able to settle their conflicts in a diplomatic way (e. g. Middle East, Northern Ireland).

Argumentationshilfen dagegen:
- It is not so much violence itself that has increased but media coverage of single violent incidents.
- The willingness to solve conflicts in an argumentative way is growing (e. g. mediators, conflict-solving work groups in schools).
- On a global scale there is a clear tendency not to solve international political problems by means of wars but by negotiations (e. g. the unification of Germany, fall of the Iron Curtain).

Formulierungsvorschläge für beide Schlussvarianten:

dafür:
Even though it is true that many everyday conflicts are of course solved by arguments instead of violence, there is no denying the fact that nowadays violent incidents are on the increase. If we don't oppose this trend there is a great danger of our losing the ability to use arguments instead of fists and weapons to solve our problems.

dagegen:
After weighing up all these arguments one must agree that, even if examples of violence instead of arguments can frequently be observed, it is nevertheless not people's usual way of solving problems. Taking into consideration all the conflicts occurring every day, it is an exaggeration to say that today's conflicts are mainly solved by means of violence.

Tipp
siehe S. 12

Meinungsthema

3. A good education – a safe way to a successful future? Give your opinion.

Formulierungsvorschlag zur Einleitung:

Many parents would do anything to give their children the best education possible because they are convinced that a good education is sure to lead to a successful future.

Argumentionshilfen dafür:

- A good education contributes to one's self-confidence.
- Good schools help pupils to develop certain skills and abilities which can pave the way to success.
- Better education provides better chances on the job market and a good job is often the basis for a successful life.

Argumentationshilfen dagegen:

- Even nowadays there are lots of men and women who have managed to lead a successful life without having completed their education.
- In our fast-changing world, spontaneity and flexibility are often more important than exams, diplomas and good marks.
- Leading a successful life also depends on factors that have nothing whatsoever to do with education, such as personal relationships, happiness or contentedness.

Formulierungsvorschläge für beide Schlussvarianten:

dafür:

Nowadays a good education is vital for success in securing a good job and leading a full and happy everyday life. As far as I am concerned, the American Dream of rags to riches is nothing more than a myth.

dagegen:

Considering the fact that there are people who have managed to become successful with barely any education at all it is absurd to claim that education is the key to success. Nowadays, in an ever-changing society, there are no safe ways to anything at all.

Nachdem er den Wetterbericht angehört hatte, hatte Frankies Papa (1) auf der Suche nach einer Nachrichtensendung aus Belfast am Bordradio gedreht. Frankie wusste schon eine ganze Menge über die *Unruhen*. Sie hatten Männer wie Connies und seinen eigenen Papa zu Feinden werden lassen. Und in letzter Zeit hatten sich diese Unruhen verstärkt. So sehr er auch das Jesuskind und die Jungfrau Maria liebte, er konnte dennoch nicht ergründen/verstehen, warum der Ort, an dem eine Familie Gottesdienst feiert, so einen großen Unterschied machen konnte. Hatten er und Connie nicht dasselbe helle ingwerfarbene Haar, dieselben schelmischen blauen Augen und denselben blassen, von Sommersprossen bedeckten Körper/dieselbe … bedeckte Haut, der/die in der Sommersonne in heftigem Rot (2) brannte?

„… sagen, dass Zusammenstöße zwischen katholischen Anwohnern entlang der Falls Road und der Armee eskalierten, nachdem ein Gummigeschoss ein siebenjähriges Mädchen getötet hatte (3)", verlas der Sprecher mit monotoner Stimme. „Es wurde von einem britischen Soldaten abgefeuert, um einen katholischen Protestmarsch aufzulösen, der in Gewalt auszuarten drohte."

„Schwachsinn!" knurrte Frankies Papa. „Er ist jetzt in Gewalt ausgeartet, ihr verfluchten Arschlöcher. Verdamm' euch allesamt in das tiefste Loch der Hölle."

(1) Hier wurde die vertrautere Form *Dad*, die hier auch noch umgangssprachlich zu *da* abgekürzt wird, mit einer entsprechenden deutschen Form übersetzt. Natürlich kann man es auch bei der neutraleren Form „Vater" belassen, oder sogar auf das englische *Dad* zurückgreifen, das hierzulande hinreichend bekannt ist.

(2) Der englische Begriff *angry red* kann hier nicht wörtlich übersetzt werden.

(3) Im Deutschen muss nach „nachdem" das Plusquamperfekt stehen.

3. Dead Poets' Society

3.1. Text und Aufgaben

Zu bearbeitender Text

It is 1959 and some boys are studying together at an elite school in New England. The new term has just started.

There was another knock on the door. "It's open," Neil called. But it wasn't another of their buddies this time.

"Father," Neil stammered, his face turning white. "I thought you'd left!"

The boys jumped to their feet. "Mr. Perry," Meeks, Charlie, and Knox
5   said in unison.

"Keep your seats, boys," Neil's father said as he walked briskly into the room. "How's it going?"

"Fine, sir. Thank you," they answered.

Mr. Perry stood face to face with Neil, who shuffled uncomfortably.
10 "Neil, I've decided that you're taking too many extracurricular activities. I've spoken to Mr. Nolan about it, and he's agreed to let you work on the school annual *next* year," he said, and then walked toward the door.

"But, Father," Neil cried. "I'm the assistant editor!"

"I'm sorry, Neil," Mr. Perry replied stiffly.
15 "But, Father, it's not fair. I …,"

Mr. Perry's eyes glared at Neil, who stopped midsentence. Then he opened the door and pointed to Neil to leave the room.

"Fellows, would you excuse us a minute?" he asked politely. Mr. Perry followed Neil, closing the door behind him.
20 His eyes raging, Mr. Perry hissed at his son. "I will *not* be disputed in public, do you understand me?"

"Father," Neil said lamely, "I wasn't disputing you. I …"

"When you've finished medical school and you're on your own, you can do as you please. Until then, you will listen to ME!"
25 Neil looked at the floor. "Yes, sir. I'm sorry."

"You know what this means to your mother, don't you?" Mr. Perry said.

"Yes, sir." Neil stood silent in front of his father. His resolve always crumbled under the threats of guilt and punishment. "Oh well, you know me," Neil said, filling the pause. "Always taking on too much."
30 "Good boy. Call us if you need anything." He turned without further comment and walked off. Neil looked after his father, feeling overwhelmed with frustration and anger. Why did he always let his father get to him like that?

He opened the door to his room and walked back in. The boys tried to
35 look as if nothing had happened, each waiting for the other to speak. Finally Charlie broke the silence.

"Why doesn't he ever let you do what you want?" he asked.

"And why don't you just tell him off! It couldn't get any worse," Knox added.

40 Neil wiped his eyes. "Oh, that's rich," he sneered. "Like you tell YOUR parents off, Mr. Future Lawyer and Mr. Future Banker!" The boys studied their shoes as Neil stormed around the room angrily. He ripped the school annual achievement pin from his blazer and hurled it furiously at his desk.

45 "Wait a minute," Knox said, walking toward Neil. "I don't let my parents walk on me." "Yeah," Neil laughed. "You just do everything they say! You'll be in daddy's law firm as sure as I'm standing here." He turned to Charlie who was sprawled across Neil's bed. "And you'll be approving loans till you croak!"

50 "Okay," Charlie admitted. "So I don't like it any more than you do. I'm just saying ..."

"Then don't tell me how to talk to my father when you're the same way," Neil snapped. "All right?"

"All right," Knox sighed. "Jesus, what are you gonna do?"

55 "What I have to do. Chuck the annual. I have no choice."

"I certainly wouldn't lose any sleep over it," Meeks said cheerfully, "It's just a bunch of people trying to impress Nolan."

Neil slammed his suitcase shut and slumped onto his bed. "What do I care about any of it anyhow""

From: N. H. Kleinbaum, Bantam Books, New York, 1993, pp. 14–17

I. Language/Form

1. Paraphrase the underlined expression: "And why don't you just <u>tell</u> him <u>off</u>!" (line 38).

2. In what way does the father's language reflect that he has the say in the family? Give two examples from the text.

II. Comprehension

(Use your own words as far as possible.)

1. What is the reason for the argument between Neil and his father?

2. Describe the relationship between Neil and his father. Give evidence from the text.

3. How do the boys react when Mr. Perry has gone?

III. Comment

(Choose one of the following topics.)

1. "When you've finished medical school and you're on your own, you can do as you please. Until then, you will listen to ME!" (lines 23–24). Discuss whether authority and subordination are a good basis for family relationships.

2. Are good schoolmarks a guarantee for getting the job you dream of? Give your opinion.

3. Parents have the permanent right to interfere with their children's lives. Discuss.

IV. Translation

Translate lines 1–17 (from: "There was …" up to "… to leave the room.").

3.2. Lösungsweg und Lösungsvorschläge

I. Language/Form

Aufgaben zu Sprache und Stil

1. Paraphrase the underlined expression: "And why don't you just <u>tell</u> him <u>off</u>!" (line 38).

Why don't you just give him a piece of your mind?

2. In what way does the father's language reflect that he has the say in the family? Give two examples from the text.

Antwort im ganzen Text verteilt

Überzeugendste Beispiele aussuchen

Hier werden mehr als die verlangten zwei Beispiele angegeben, damit Sie sich für die beiden entscheiden können, die Sie am überzeugendsten finden.

Stoffsammlung:
- "I've decided that you're taking too many extracurricular activities." (l. 10)
- "I will *not* be disputed in public, do you understand me?" (ll. 20–21)
- "When you've finished medical school and you're on your own, you can do as you please. Until then, you will listen to ME." (ll. 23–24)

Formulierungshilfe:
He uses very authoritarian language, takes decisions for his son by saying "I've decided that you're taking too many extracurricular activities" (l. 10) and makes arrangements for him. His leading position in the family is reflected by his emphasizing the first person singular as he does when telling Neil, "Until then, you will listen to ME." (l. 24). By emphasizing certain parts of his speech, such as "I will *not* be disputed in public, do you understand me?" (ll. 20–21) he wants to make sure that nobody will undermine his authority.

II. Comprehension

(Use your own words as far as possible.)

Antwort im ersten Teil
des Textes

1. What is the reason for the argument between Neil and his father?

Stoffsammlung:
- In his father's view Neil is taking too many extracurricular activities.
- His father stops him from working for the school annual.
- Neil thinks this is not fair because he is the assistant editor.
- Neil disputes his father in public.

Formulierungsvorschlag:
The starting point of the argument between Neil and his father is the fact that Mr Perry thinks his son is taking part in too many activities apart from his regular school subjects. When he talks to him he has already seen to it that Neil is no longer allowed to work for the school annual. Neil, however tells his father that this is not fair as he is nothing less than the assistant editor. Mr Perry does not like his son to contradict him in the presence of others and becomes angry.

**Tipp
siehe S. 9**

Textstellen belegen

Antwort im ersten Teil
des Textes

2. Describe the relationship between Neil and his father. Give evidence from the text.

Stoffsammlung:
Neil:
- is afraid of his father: "… his face turning white." (l. 3); "… shuffled uncomfortably …" (l. 9)
- is unable to put up resistance to his father: "His resolve always crumbled under the threats of guilt and punishment." (ll. 27–28); "Why did he always let his father get to him like that?" (ll. 32–33)
- says things he does not really mean in order to satisfy his father: "Oh well, you know me […] Always taking on too much." (ll. 28–29)

Mr Perry:
- does not show any affection for his son: Even when he pretends to show emotions, his gestures and his tone contradict his words: "'I'm sorry, Neil,' Mr Perry replied stiffly." (l. 14); "'Good boy. […]' He turned without further comment …" (ll. 30–31)
- oppresses his son: "I will not be disputed in public, …" (ll. 20–21); "Until then you will listen to ME!" (l. 24)

Formulierungsvorschlag:

The underlying reason for the conflict between Neil and h s father is their general relationship which is characterized by Mr Perry's authoritarian and oppressive style of education: He hates being "disputed in public" (ll. 20–21) and expects Neil to obey his father's will (l. 24). In addition to that he does not show any real affection for his son. Even when he pretends to show emotions, his gestures and his tone contradict his words, as, for example, when he says sorry, which he does in a very stiff way (l. 14). After that, Mr Perry calls Neil a "good boy" (l. 30), but then turns away "without further comment" (ll. 30–31).

Neil's reactions reveal how much he fears his father: His face turns white (l. 3) and he shuffles uncomfortably (l. 9) when he sees him. Furthermore, he is unable to put up resistance to his father: "His resolve always crumbled under the threats of guilt and punishment." (ll. 27–28), even if Neil is sorry about the fact that he always lets "his father get to him like that? (ll. 32–33). A consequence of Neil's fear of his father is the fact that in the end he says things he does not really mean, in order to satisfy his father: "Oh well, you know me […] Always taking on too much." (ll. 28–29).

3. How do the boys react when Mr Perry has gone?

Antwort im zweiten Teil

Stoffsammlung:
- They try to look as if nothing has happened and do not talk.
- Charlie and Knox begin to reproach Neil for giving in.
- They argue about the relationships between them and their own parents.
- They admit that they are no better than Neil.
- Meeks tries to convince Neil that he has not really lost anything.

Formulierungsvorschlag:

When Mr Perry has gone, the boys initially seem to be embarrassed, pretending that nothing has happened and do not talk to each other for a while. After that, Charlie and Knox begin to reproach Neil for giving in too easily. Then, however, Neil tells them that they are no better in pleasing their own parents, something which in the end they are forced to admit. Meeks finally declares, though not very convincingly, that working on the school annual would not have been very desirable anyway.

III. Comment

Choose <u>one</u> of the following topics.

1. **"When you've finished medical school and you're on your own, you can do as you please. Until then, you will listen to ME!" (ll. 23–24). Discuss whether authority and subordination are a good basis for family relationships.**

Formulierungsvorschlag zur Einleitung:
There will always be parents who insist on their children obeying them as long as they live in their household. They demand that their children do as they say and they tolerate no "ifs" and "buts". But are parental authority and domination really a good basis for family relationships?

Argumentationshilfen dafür:
- A set of rules obeyed by all family members can help to reduce stress and conflicts within a family.
- The rules children need for guidance within the family can only be upheld by means of a certain amount of authority. Otherwise children would constantly hurt other family members' feelings without even noticing it.
- Without authority children would not be able to distinguish between right and wrong.

Argumentationshilfen dagegen:
- How democratic can a family be if not every single family member is allowed to express freely what he or she thinks because the authoritarian head of the family always insists on his or her opinion?
- Children who know nothing but authority and subordination in their families will never learn how to make decisions on their own.
- Too much authority is often achieved by means of physical and mental violence at the expense of love and affection, the real basis for harmonic family relationships.

Formulierungsvorschläge für beide Schlussvarianten:

dafür:
Of course it is true that too much authority is no longer in keeping with the times as it does not leave any scope for personal development. Yet, in my opinion, a certain amount of authority is necessary to provide for a reliable structure within a family thus preparing children for the authoritarian structures they may encounter outside the family in their future lives.

dagegen:
Taking all the pros and cons into account I must admit that a certain amount of authority and subordination in education has some indisputable advantages. Still I am convinced that a democratic family structure does not only contribute to harmonic family relationships but also prepares the children for their lives as adults in a democratic society.

2. Are good schoolmarks a guarantee for getting the job you dream of? Give your opinion.

Tipp
siehe S. 12

Formulierungsvorschlag zur Einleitung:

Meinungsthema

Generations of parents have urged pupils to study hard at school, pointing out that only good marks would secure them the job of their dreams. Does this belief hold up to careful examination?

Argumentationshilfen dafür:
- Good schoolmarks are a precondition for many jobs, for example those that require university degrees.
- Good marks usually help to increase people's self-esteem which helps them to appear more self-confident in job interviews etc.
- When you apply for a job one of the first things you will have to hand in is still the school diploma.

Argumentationshilfen dagegen:
- There are jobs for which the outer appearance is at least as important as school marks, for example flight attendant, model etc.
- There are many dream jobs which require a high amount of creativity which is not reflected by school marks.
- Many employers put more emphasis on people's character (self-confidence, commitment, flexibility, reliability etc.) than on their marks.

Formulierungsvorschlag für den Schluss:

Trotz einiger Pro-Argumente muss man davon ausgehen, dass gute Schulnoten allein keinesfalls eine ausdrückliche Garantie für den Traumjob sein können. Deshalb bieten wir hier nur **eine** Schlussvariante.

Nur eine Schluss-variante

Of course it is true that many careers require a sound education, but there are just as many other qualifications that are important to get a good job. To put it in a nutshell, good marks are by no means a guarantee you will get the job you dream of, but they may be <u>one</u> precondition for many jobs.

Tipp
siehe S. 13

Dialektisches Thema

3. Parents have the permanent right to interfere with their children's lives. Discuss.

Formulierungsvorschlag zur Einleitung:

There are lots of parents who do not want to, or are not able to, realize that their children have become adults with the right to lead their own lives, make their own decisions and take responsibility for themselves. They think it makes them loving and caring parents if they continuously interfere in their offspring's lives. To their dismay, however, many adult sons and daughters do not think their parents have the right to do so.

Argumentationshilfe dafür:

- Parents have the right and even the duty to interfere in their children's lives to a certain extent as long as their sons and daughters are not old enough to make all important decisions on their own.

Argumentationshilfen dagegen:

- If parents continuously interfere with their children's lives, their sons and daughters will never learn to cope with the difficulties of life on their own.
- Children have to stand on their own two feet, in good times and bad, in order to develop as individuals.
- Every adult has the right to lead his or her own life without anybody's interference.

Formulierungsvorschlag für den Schluss:

It is reassuring for all of us, both in childhood and as adults, to know that we have parents who will always be there and lend a helping hand when needed. Once the children have reached a certain state of maturity, however, parents should rather be friends and advisors, but of course only when asked for help. If parents think they have a permanent right to interfere, they will sooner or later see the bonds with their children destroyed.

Es klopfte noch einmal an der Tür. „Es ist offen", rief Neil. Aber diesmal war es nicht wieder einer ihrer Kumpels. „Vater", stammelte Neil, und sein Gesicht wurde weiß. „Ich dachte, du wärst schon gegangen." Die Jungs sprangen auf. „Mr. Perry", sagten Meeks, Charlie und Knox gleichzeitig/wie aus einem Munde. „Bleibt sitzen, Jungs", sagte Neils Vater, als er forsch/energisch den Raum betrat. „Wie läuft's?" „Gut, Sir. Danke", antworteten sie.

Mr. Perry stand Neil, der unbehaglich mit den Füßen scharte, unmittelbar gegenüber. „Neil, ich habe beschlossen, dass du an zu vielen Aktivitäten außerhalb deines Stundenplans teilnimmst. Ich habe mit Mr. Nolan darüber gesprochen, und er ist damit einverstanden dich *nächstes* Jahr am Jahrbuch der Schule mitarbeiten zu lassen", sagte er und ging dann in Richtung Tür.

„Aber Vater", rief Neil, „ich bin der stellvertretende Herausgeber!" „Es tut mir Leid", antwortete Mr. Perry steif.

„Aber, Vater, das ist nicht fair. Ich …"

Mr. Perry starrte Neil, der mitten im Satz verstummte, mit zornigen Augen (1) an. Dann öffnete er die Tür und bedeutete ihm, dass er das Zimmer verlassen sollte.

(1) wörtl.: „Mr. Perrys Augen starrten Neil zornig an."

4. Pride and Prejudice

4.1. Text und Aufgaben

It is a truth universally acknowledged, that a single man in possession of a good fortune, must be in want of a wife.

However little known the feelings or views of such a man may be on his first entering a neighbourhood, this truth is so well fixed in the minds of
5 the surrounding families, that he is considered as the rightful property of some one or other of their daughters.

'My dear Mr Bennet,' said his lady to him one day, 'have you heard that Netherfield Park is let at last?'

Mr Bennet replied that he had not.
10 'But it is,' returned she; 'for Mrs Long has just been here, and she told me all about it.'

Mr Bennet made no answer.

'Do not you want to know who has taken it?' cried his wife impatiently.

'You want to tell me, and I have no objection to hearing it.' This was in-
15 vitation enough.

'Why, my dear, you must know, Mrs Long says that Netherfield is taken by a young man of large fortune from the north of England; that he came down on Monday in a chaise and four to see the place, and was so much delighted with it that he agreed with Mr Morris immediately; that he is to
20 take possession before Michaelmas, and some of his servants are to be in the house by the end of next week.'

'What is his name?'

'Bingley.'

'Is he married or single?'
25 'Oh! single, my dear, to be sure! A single man of large fortune; four or five thousand a year. What a fine thing for our girls!'

'How so? how can it affect them?'

'My dear Mr Bennet, replied his wife, 'how can you be so tiresome! You must know that I am thinking of his marrying one of them.'
30 'Is that his design in settling here?'

'Design! nonsense, how can you talk so! But it is very likely that he *may* fall in love with one of them, and therefore you must visit him as soon as he comes.'

'I see no occasion for that. You and the girls may go, or you may send
35 them by themselves, which perhaps will be still better, for as you are as handsome as any of them, Mr Bingley might like you the best of the party.'

'My dear, you flatter me. I certainly *have* had my share of beauty, but I do not pretend to be any thing extraordinary now. When a woman has five
40 grown up daughters, she ought to give over thinking of her own beauty.'

' In such cases, a woman has not often much beauty to think of.'

'But, my dear, you must indeed go and see Mr Bingley when he comes into the neighbourhood.'

'It is more than I engage for, I assure you.'

45 'But consider your daughters. Only think what an establishment it would be for one of them. Sir William and Lady Lucas are determined to go, merely on that account, for in general you know they visit no new comers. Indeed you must go, for it will be impossible for *us* to visit him, if you do not.'

50 'You are over scrupulous surely. I dare say Mr Bingley will be very glad to see you; and I will send a few lines by you to assure him of my hearty consent to his marrying which ever he chuses of the girls; though I must throw in a good word for my little Lizzy.'

'I desire you will do no such thing. Lizzy is not a bit better than the oth-
55 ers; and I am sure she is not half so handsome as Jane, nor half so good humoured as Lydia. But you are always giving *her* the preference.'

'They have none of them much to recommend them,' replied he; 'they are all silly and ignorant like other girls; but Lizzy has something more of quickness than her sisters.'

60 'Mr Bennet, how can you abuse your own children in such a way? You take delight in vexing me. You have no compassion on my poor nerves.'

'You mistake me, my dear. I have a high respect – for your nerves. They are my old friends. I have heard you mention them with consideration these twenty years at least.'

65 'Ah! you do not know what I suffer.'

'But I hope you will get over it, and live to see many young men of four thousand a year come into the neighbourhood.'

'It will be no use to us, if twenty such should come since you will not visit them.'

70 'Depend upon it, my dear, that when there are twenty, I will visit them all.'

Mr Bennet was so odd a mixture of quick parts, sarcastic humour, reserve, and caprice, that the experience of three and twenty years had been insufficient to make his wife understand his character. *Her* mind
75 was less difficult to develope . She was a woman of mean understanding, little information, and uncertain temper. When she was discontented she fancied herself nervous. The business of her life was to get her daughters married; its solace was visiting and news.

From: Jane Austen, *Pride and Prejudice,* 1813

Note: The language of the text, esp. punctuation, spelling and syntax, has not been modernised.

18 *chaise and four:* a carriage drawn by four horses • 25–26 *four or five thousand [pounds]:* the equivalent of several hundred thousand pounds today • 44 *engage for* (archaic): promise • 45 *establishment:* a financially desirable marriage • 52 *chuses (archaic):* chooses • 73 *quick parts* (archaic): keen intellect • 76 *develope* (archaic): understand • 76 *mean:* here: inferior

I. Questions on the text

Read all the questions first, then answer them in the given order.
Use your own words as far as is appropriate.

1. What news has Mrs Long brought and why is it important for the Bennet family?

2. Describe the social background, including social conventions, of the characters presented in this chapter. Give evidence from the text.

3. What concept of marriage seems to be prevalent in this social group?

4. Analyse the strategies Mrs Bennet uses in her attempt to persuade her husband.

5. Compare Mr and Mrs Bennet's attitudes towards their daughters.

6. Show that Mr Bennet is indeed a man of 'sarcastic humour' (l. 82). Give three examples from the dialogue and explain them.

7. What impression of Mrs Bennet is conveyed to the reader? How is this achieved? (Consider narrative perspective, mode of presentation and tone.)

II. Composition
Choose o n e of the following topics.

1. 'The love of money is the root of all evil.' Discuss.

2. Do women today enjoy equal status and equal opportunities?

3. The relationship between man and woman has often been dealt with in literature. Choose one work by an English-speaking author and show how this topic is treated.

III. Translation

Translate the following text into German:

The first novelist in English literature to understand what the novel should not attempt, and what it can do supremely well, was Jane Austen. Her restricted subject-matter – the small section of society that she treats, the narrow range of her settings has been attributed to the restricted experience of life of this unmarried clergyman's daughter. The real explanation is artistic. She knew that significant experience did not always or necessarily arise from extraordinary conditions, that conversations about what is commonplace may reveal character even more effectively than conversations about what is exceptional, and that the depth of a reader's impression of a story is proportionate to the extent to which he has found it convincing.

Later novelists, writing under different social conditions, enriched the art by breaking the limits she imposed on herself, but it would be a mistake to assume from this that her art was excessively conventional. It was Jane Austen who first brought to light what was to be one of the principal themes of the later-19th-century novel: the predicament of the individual, particularly of the woman, who requires personal fulfilment in society, and finds that society imposes far more obstacles than opportunities for realizing this desire.

From: C. Gillie, *Longman Companion to English Literature,* ²1978

4.2. Lösungsweg und Lösungsvorschläge

Fragen zum Text

I. Questions on the text

Read all the questions first, then answer them in the given order.
Use your own words as far as is appropriate.

Belegstellen sind jeweils im ganzen Text zu suchen

In dieser Textaufgabe beziehen sich die Fragen zum Text nicht, wie häufig üblich, auf aufeinander folgende Textabschnitte. Die Belegstellen sind jeweils im ganzen Text zu suchen.

1. What news has Mrs Long brought and why is it important for the Bennet family?

Zweiteilige Frage! news in Z. 7–26 importance Z. 27–29

Der erste Teil dieser zweigeteilten Frage bezieht sich auf die Neuigkeiten (Z. 7–26), der zweite Teil soll darlegen, warum die Neuigkeiten wichtig für die Familie Bennet sind (Z. 27–29).

Stoffsammlung:
news:
- Netherfield Park is let at last.
- It is taken by a young man of large fortune.
- He has been here to see the place.
- He is unmarried.

importance for the Bennet family:
- Mrs Bennet is thinking of him marrying one of her daughters.

Formulierungsvorschlag:
Mrs Long has brought the news that a young, rich and unmarried man is going to move to Netherfield Park, a neighbouring estate. He has already been there to see the place which he liked so much that he intends to move in soon.
This is of relevance for the Bennet family as Mrs Bennet hopes he will fall in love with and marry one of her daughters.

Zweiteilige Frage!

Belegstellen im ganzen Text

Fundstellen belegen (vgl Teil A)

2. Describe the social background, including social conventions, of the characters presented in this chapter. Give evidence from the text.

Auch diese Frage ist zweigeteilt, da sowohl der soziale Hintergrund der Familie als auch Konventionen beschrieben werden sollen. Die entsprechenden Informationen sind im ganzen Text zu finden und müssen auch explizit belegt werden.

Stoffsammlung:

social background
- They belong to the upper middle class.
- They know noble people (Sir William and Lady Lucas) (l. 46).
- They must have a certain amount of wealth to be able to hope that Mr Bingley would want to marry one of their daughters (ll. 28–29).
- They use very formal language even in their private conversations ("My dear Mr Bennet" (l. 28); "I desire you will do no such thing" (ll. 54).

social conventions
- The head of the family has to meet newcomers first in order to arrange a meeting with the other members of his family (ll. 32–33).
- Marrying their children into money is very important for every family.

Tipp
siehe S. 11

Formulierungsvorschlag:

The Bennets' social background and the social conventions they live by can only be inferred implicitly. From the Bennets' acquaintances and the way they talk to each other one can conclude that they belong to the upper middle class. They associate with noble people such as "Sir William and Lady Lucas" (l. 46), and use quite formal language even in their private conversations. Mrs Bennet, for example, calls her husband "My dear Mr Bennet" (l. 28) and expresses her disapproval of his behaviour with the words "I desire you will do no such thing" (l. 54).

The Bennets' social status requires the fulfillment of certain social conventions, for example marrying their children into money: Marrying a "man of large fortune" (l. 25) would be "a fine thing for our girls" (l. 26) and an "establishment" (ll. 52–53).

Moreover, it is of paramount importance that the head of a family meets promising "new comers" (ll. 47–48) before a meeting with the other family members can be arranged. This is why Mrs Bennet says: "… it will be impossible for us to visit him if you do not." (ll. 48–49)

3. What concept of marriage seems to be prevalent in this social group?

Antwort nur aus der Konversation zu erschließen

Stoffsammlung:
- The aim of every rich and unmarried man is to get married.
- The aim of all women is to get married.
- The aim of all parents is to marry their girls into money.
- Parents arrange their children's marriages.

Formulierungsvorschlag:

Being married is one of the most important social aims of the upper middle class described in "Pride and Prejudice". The prevalent concept of marriage is mainly focussed on money: Women want to get married to secure their financial status, parents want their children, especially their girls, to marry in order to ensure their financial security. This is why they choose their daughters' spouses.

4. Analyse the strategies Mrs Bennet uses in her attempt to persuade her husband.

Antwort im gesamten Text zu finden

Stoffsammlung:
- arouses his interest ("Have you heard that Netherfield Park is let at last?") (ll. 7–8)
- reacts impatiently when her husband does not answer
- tells everything and then switches to her actual aim: her husband should visit Mr Bingley
- When he does not react to her demand she insists on it by repeating her request ("Indeed you must go.") (l. 48).
- She insinuates that he does not show enough consideration for her ("You have no compassion on my poor nerves." (l. 61).
- She wants to create a guilty conscience ("You do not know what I suffer." (l. 66).

Formulierungshilfe:
To begin with Mrs Bennet tries to arouse her husband's interest in the new neighbour by asking the seemingly unimportant question "Have you heard that Netherfield Park is let at last?" (ll. 7–8). To her disapproval, he does not show any interest which makes her react impatiently (l. 13). Then she tells Mr Bennet the news and makes a clever switch towards her actual intention, i. e. to make her husband visit the new neighbour Mr Bingley. When he is reluctant to do so, she insists on her desire by repeating her request several times: "… you must indeed go …" (l. 42), "Indeed you must go …" (l. 48). The next step of her strategy is to insinuate that he does not show enough consideration for her: "You have no compassion on my poor nerves." (l. 61). Finally, she even wants to instil a sense of guilt into him by saying "Ah! you do not know what I suffer." (l. 66)
To sum up, Mrs Bennet makes use of a series of different clever steps that are all part of her strategy to get her husband to do as she wants.

5. Compare Mr and Mrs Bennet's attitudes towards their daughters.

Antwort in den Zeilen 54–59

Stoffsammlung:
Mr Bennet:
- favours Lizzy
- considers all of them silly and ignorant like other girls
- thinks that Lizzy "has something more of quickness" than her sisters
Mrs Bennet:
- considers Lizzy not a bit better than the others
- considers Jane handsome and Lydia good humoured
- wants them to get married

Formulierungsvorschlag:

Mr Bennet does not think very highly of girls in general because he considers them "silly and ignorant" (l. 58). However, he favours his daughter Lizzy because to his mind she is more intelligent than her sisters.

His wife, on the other hand, has no favourite daughter even though she sees differences in their characters and appearances. For example, she considers one of her daughters more handsome whereas the other one is more good humoured. No matter what she thinks of every single one of her daughters, the most important thing for her is to find them suitable husbands.

6. Show that Mr Bennet is indeed a man of "sarcastic humour" (l. 73). Give three examples from the dialogue and explain them.

Wie immer bei Fragen nach Stilmitteln empfiehlt es sich hier, den Begriff „Sarkasmus" kurz zu erklären. Die Beispiele sind auf den gesamten Text verteilt und müssen zitiert werden (vgl. Teil A).

Tipp siehe S. 9

„Sarkasmus" erklären (vgl. Teil C)

Antwort im ganzen Text

Belegstellen angeben

Stoffsammlung:

- sarcasm: bitter, often ironic remarks aimed at hurting people's feelings
- "You want to tell me, and I have no objection to hearing it." (l. 14)
- "Is that his design in settling here?" (l. 30)
- "… for as you are as handsome as any of them, Mr Bingley might like you the best of the party." (ll. 35–37)
- "… I will send a few lines by you to assure him of my hearty consent to his marrying which ever he chuses of the girls;" (ll. 51–52)
- "But I hope you will get over it, and live to see many young men of four thousand a year come into the neighbourhood." (ll. 67–68)

Formulierungshilfe:

Mr Bennet's speech is full of sarcasm and bitter irony that is meant to hurt his wife's feelings. In the beginning, for example, when Mrs Bennet insists on telling him the exciting news about Mr Bingley, he answers: "You want to tell me, and I have no objection to hearing it." (l. 14). By saying so he shows that he is not actually interested in what she is going to tell him; he simply endures her chattering. Once more he shows that he is not interested in his wife's plans to marry off their daughters when, instead of actually paying Mr Bingley a visit, he sarcastically offers to send him a letter allowing him to marry any of his daughters. Finally, he tells her "I hope you will get over it" (l. 67) and thus pretends to take her sufferings seriously, when in reality he is only poking fun at her.

Zweiteilige Frage

Antwort auf den
gesamten Text verteilt

7. What impression of Mrs Bennet is conveyed to the reader? How is this achieved? (Consider narrative perspective, mode of presentation and tone.)

Der erste Teil Ihrer Antwort soll den Eindruck beschreiben, der dem Leser von Mrs. Bennet vermittelt wird, der zweite Teil untersucht die Art und Weise, wie dieses Bild vermittelt wird. Die Antwort finden Sie im ganzen Text.

Stoffsammlung:
impression of Mrs Bennet:
- silly (takes her husband's sarcastic remarks seriously)
- superficial (only interested in Mr Bingley's money, not in his character)
- narrow-minded (her main interest is getting her daughters married)
achieved by:
- omniscient narrator
- scenic mode of presentation
- ironic and sarcastic tone

Formulierungshilfe:
Jane Austen's novel *Pride and Prejudice* is presented by an omniscient narrator who, by means of his unlimited point of view, conveys an explicit image of Mrs Bennet as "a woman of mean understanding, little information, and uncertain temper." (ll. 76–77). The dialogues between Mr and Mrs Bennet, a rather scenic mode of presentation, reinforce this image in an implicit way. Mrs Bennet does not realize that most of her husband's remarks are meant in an ironic and sarcastic way, which underlines the image of her lack of intelligence. As her only interest seems to consist in getting her daughters married, she appears to be rather narrow-minded. And, what is more, she does not even care about her prospective son-in-law's character, as long as he is well-off, which reveals a certain amount of superficiality on her part.

II. Comment

Choose **o n e** of the following topics.

1. **"The love of money is the root of all evil." Discuss.**

Tipp
siehe S. 13

Dialektisches Thema

Formulierungsvorschlag zur Einleitung:
In modern society money still plays a pivotal role in many people's lives. It is accepted that even youngsters go to work to earn their own money and that some people regularly work overtime to earn more money. People are often judged by their wealth and materialism is to the fore in all walks of life. On the other hand there are voices that caution that the love of money is the root of all evil.

Argumentationshilfen dafür:
- People often neglect their families and friends for their career, i.e. for money.
- Crime is very often the result of greed (drugs, burglary etc.).
- Corruption, especially in politics, affects whole societies.

Argumentationshilfen dagegen:
- Even people who do not care about money can have a bad character; this is why the love of money cannot be the root of <u>all</u> evil.
- Not everybody who loves money is potentially evil.
- Strong characters cannot be spoilt by money.
- Money can be a good reason to increase one's efforts (job, sports etc.).

Formulierungsvorschläge für beide Schlussvarianten:

dafür:
In spite of the fact that money can be a positive factor in all our lives, there can be no denying the fact that it brings with it the potential for evil. The love of money shifts people's focus away from more important values in life and thus makes some of the columns of our society crumble.

dagegen:
Of course it is true that the love of money can spoil individual people's characters. On the whole, however, the love of money has been the source of more advantages than disadvantages for our welfare state. If nobody loved money, how could financial security for a whole society be brought about?

Tipp
siehe S. 12

Meinungsthema

2. Do women today enjoy equal status and equal opportunities?

Formulierungsvorschlag zur Einleitung:
A lot has changed since the days of Jane Austen. Women are no longer married off by their parents to wealthy strangers. Nor are they considered silly and ignorant girls who do not even have the right to vote. But have we really reached the point yet where women enjoy equal status and equal opportunities?

Argumentationshilfen dafür:
- Women are represented to a larger extent in politics than they were years ago.
- More women than ever before occupy positions involving a certain responsibility in business and industry.
- According to the law, fathers as well as mothers are allowed to take some time off and to stay at home with their small children.

Argumentationshilfen dagegen:
- There are still lots of jobs that are considered male or female jobs (for example secretaries and babysitters on the one hand and craftsmen on the other hand).
- The ratio of men and women in business and industry who occupy top positions is still a long way from 50:50.
- Most families still adhere to the traditional roles of men and women, making it impossible for women to embark on a professional career.

Formulierungsvorschläge für beide Schlussvarianten:

dafür:
There will always remain some women who think emancipation has not yet gone far enough. What they overlook, however, is the fact that, to say it quite bluntly, emancipation has reached a level which could not even have been dreamt of one hundred years ago. The remaining minor inequalities are mainly due to biological facts and may therefore never be overcome.

dagegen:
Even if a lot was achieved in the field of emancipation in the last century, there is still an enormous discrepancy between laws and reality. Many men still take their traditional male role for granted without even being aware of it. Only when men start to reconsider this role will there be a chance of achieving complete equality of the sexes one day.

3. The relationship between man and woman has often been dealt with in literature. Choose one work by an English-speaking author and show how this topic is treated.

Da der Literaturkanon in den verschiedenen Bundesländern unterschiedlich ist und nur in den seltensten Fällen bestimmte Werke überall vorgegeben sind, ist hier keine verbindliche Musterlösung möglich. Dennoch sollen Ihnen ein paar Anregungen an die Hand gegeben werden, mit deren Hilfe Sie dieses Thema bearbeiten können:

Keine verbindliche Musterlösung möglich

Auswählen könnten Sie beispielsweise Werke, in denen die Beziehung zwischen Mann und Frau in ihren verschiedenen Ausprägungen vorkommt. Beispiele für eine Liebe, der gesellschaftliche oder andere Hindernisse im Weg stehen, sind unter anderem *Romeo and Juliet*, *Love Story* oder auch *Harold and Maude*. Die problematischen Beziehungen in diesen drei Werken enden tragisch, während z. B. die Beziehung in *Pygmalion* am Ende ihre Erfüllung findet.

Eine andere Art der Ausprägung der Liebe wäre *Who is afraid of Virginia Woolf*, wo der Kampf der Geschlechter im Vordergrund steht.

Bei der Frage nach der Art und Weise, wie diese unterschiedlichen Themen behandelt werden, kann man auf die verschiedenen Darstellungsweisen (dramatisch vs. narrativ etc.) oder unterschiedlichen Erzählperspektiven etc. eingehen.

Grundsätzlich sind Ihnen bei der Behandlung dieses Themas keinerlei Grenzen gesetzt; bedenken Sie aber, dass Sie über genaue inhaltliche und formale Kenntnisse der Werke verfügen müssen, die Sie zum Bearbeiten auswählen.

III. Translation

Der erste Romanautor (1) in der englischen Literatur, der begriff, was der Roman nicht versuchen sollte und was er hervorragend kann, war Jane Austen. Ihre begrenzte Thematik – der kleine Ausschnitt der Gesellschaft, den sie behandelt, das enge Spektrum ihrer Schauplätze – all dies wurde der eingeschränkten Lebenserfahrung dieser unverheirateten Tochter eines Geistlichen (2) zugeschrieben. Die wirkliche Erklärung ist eine künstlerische. Sie wusste, dass bedeutsame Erfahrungen (3) nicht immer oder nicht unbedingt außergewöhnlichen Bedingungen entspringen, dass Gespräche über Banalitäten sogar noch effektiver etwas über den Charakter verraten können als Gespräche über Außergewöhnliches, und dass die Tiefe des Eindrucks, den eine Geschichte beim Leser hinterlässt, proportional dazu ist, wie überzeugend er sie gefunden hat.

Spätere Romanautoren, die unter anderen gesellschaftlichen Bedingungen schrieben, bereicherten die Kunst dadurch, dass sie die Beschränkungen durchbrachen, die sie sich selbst auferlegte, aber es wäre ein Fehler, deswegen anzunehmen, dass ihre Kunst übermäßig konventionell war. Es war Jane Austen, die als erste ans Licht brachte, was eines der Hauptthemen des Romans des späten 19. Jh. werden sollte: das Dilemma des Einzelnen, speziell der Frau, die nach persönlicher Erfüllung in der Gesellschaft verlangt, und die feststellt, dass die Gesellschaft ihr weitaus mehr Hindernisse in den Weg stellt als Gelegenheiten bietet (4), dieses Verlangen zu erfüllen.

(1) Leider gibt es im Deutschen keinen geschlechtsneutralen Ausdruck für *novelist*. Hier wird die männliche Form verwendet, um den Eindruck zu vermeiden, der vorliegende Text beziehe sich ausschließlich auf Autor*innen*.

(2) Theoretisch könnte sich *unmarried* auch auf *clergyman* beziehen, was jedoch nicht den Tatsachen entspricht.

(3) *experience* ist im Englischen unzählbar, wird hier jedoch sinnvollerweise mit dem deutschen Plural wiedergegeben.

(4) Im Gegensatz zum Englischen gibt es im Deutschen kein Verb, welches man sowohl im Zusammenhang mit „Hindernissen" als auch „Möglichkeiten" verwenden kann.

Sachtexte

1. The Birth of the Global Nation

1.1. Text und Aufgaben

All countries are basically social arrangements, accommodations to changing circumstances. No matter how permanent and even sacred they may seem at any one time, in fact they are all artificial and temporary.

5 The forerunner of the nation was a prehistoric band clustered around a fire beside a river in a valley. Its members had a language, a set of supernatural beliefs and a repertoire of legends about their ancestors. Eventually they forged primitive weapons and set off over the mountain, mumbling phrases that could be loosely translated as having something to do
10 with "vital national interests" and "manifest destiny." When they reached the next valley, they massacred and enslaved some weaker band of people they found clustered around some smaller fire and thus became the world's first imperialists.

The main goal driving the process of political expansion and consolida-
15 tion was conquest. The big absorbed the small, the strong the weak. National might made international right. Such a world was in a more or less constant state of war.

In the 18th century the Enlightenment – represented by Rousseau in France, Hume in Scotland, Kant in Germany, Paine and Jefferson in the
20 US – gave rise to the idea that all human beings are born equal and should, as citizens, enjoy certain basic liberties and rights, including that of choosing their leaders. Once there was a universal ideology to govern the conduct of nations toward their own people, it was more reasonable to imagine a compact governing nations' behaviour toward one another.
25 In 1795 Kant advocated a "peaceful league of democracies."

But it has taken the events of our own wondrous and terrible century to clinch the case for world government. With the advent of electricity, radio and air travel, the planet has become smaller than ever, its commercial life freer, its nations more interdependent and its conflicts blood-
30 ier. The price of settling international disputes by force was rapidly becoming too high to the victors, not to mention the vanquished. That

Zu bearbeitender Text

conclusion should have been clear enough at the battle of the Somme in 1916; by the destruction of Hiroshima in 1945, it was unavoidable.

35 Once again great minds thought alike: Einstein, Gandhi, Toynbee and Camus all favored giving primacy to interests higher than those of the nation. So, finally, did many statesmen. Each world war inspired the creation of an international organization, the League of Nations in the 1920s and the United Nations in the '40s.

40 The cold war also saw the European Community pioneer the kind of regional cohesion that may pave the way for globalism. Meanwhile, the free world formed multilateral financial institutions that depend on member states' willingness to give up a degree of sovereignty. The International Monetary Fund can virtually dictate fiscal policies, even including how much tax a government should levy on its citizens. The General 45 Agreement on Tariffs and Trade regulates how much duty a nation can charge on imports. These organizations can be seen as the protoministries of trade, finance and development for a united world.

The internal affairs of a nation used to be off limits to the world community. Now the principle of "humanitarian intervention" is gaining accep- 50 tance. A turning point came in April 1991, when the UN Security Council authorized allied troops to assist starving Kurds in northern Iraq.

Globalization has also contributed to the spread of terrorism, drug trafficking, AIDS and environmental degradation. But because those threats are more than any one nation can cope with on its own, they constitute an 55 incentive for international cooperation.

However limited its accomplishments, last month's Earth Summit in Rio signified the participants' acceptance of what Maurice Strong, the main impressario of the event, called "the transcending sovereignty of nature": since the by-products of industrial civilization cross borders, so must the 60 authority to deal with them.

Humanity has discovered, through much trial and horrendous error, that differences need not divide. Switzerland is made up of four nationalities crammed into an area considerably smaller than what used to be Yugoslavia. The air in the Alps is no more conducive to comity than the air 65 in the Balkans. Switzerland has thrived, while Yugoslavia has failed because of what Kant realized 200 years ago: to be in peaceful league with one another, people – and peoples – must have the benefits of democracy.

The best mechanism for democracy, whether at the level of the multinational state or that of the planet as a whole, is not an all-powerful cen-

70 tralized superstate, but a federation, a union of separate states that allo-
    cate certain powers to a central government while retaining many others
    for themselves.

    As for humanity as a whole, if federally united, we won't really be so
    very far from those much earlier ancestors, the ones huddled around that
75 primeval fire beside the river; it's just that by then the whole world will
    be our valley.

From: Time, July 20, 1992

10 *manifest destiny:* 19th century belief that the people of the US were chosen by God to in-
habit the entire North American continent • 32 long battle on the River Somme in France,
with extremely heavy losses on both sides • 34 *Arnold Joseph Toynbee* (1889-1975): British
historian • 35 *Albert Camus* (1913-1960): French writer • 64 *comity:* friendly respectful behaviour between groups for their mutual benefit

I. Questions on the text

Read all the questions first, then answer them in the given order. Use your own words as far as is appropriate.

1. In what way was the prehistoric tribe the writer refers to in line 5 "the forerunner of the nation"? Why does he call its members "the world's first imperialists" (line 13)?

2. Which philosophical arguments prior to the 20th century provided the basis for the idea of a harmonious relationship between nations?

3. Outline the causes for the establishment of supranational organizations during the first half of the present century.

4. What progress has been achieved on an economic level? Explain its national and global implications.

5. What decisive change took place in 1991?

6. What points does the writer try to prove by using Switzerland and Yugoslavia as concrete examples?

7. What kind of reader is the article aimed at? Consider the structure and style of the text.

II. Composition

Choose o n e of the following topics.

1. Separatism versus world government. How do you explain these opposing trends?

2. "Nature knows no frontiers." Explain the topicality of this sentence with reference to environmental problems.

3. Education for peace. What could be done in schools to further this idea?

III. Translation

Translate the following text into German:

If men have not hitherto realized the extent of their planetary interdependence, it was in part at least because, in clear, precise, physical and scientific fact, it did not exist. The new insights of our fundamental condition can also become the insights of our survival.

The first step toward devising a strategy for planet Earth is for the nations to accept a collective responsibility for discovering much more about the natural system and how it is affected by man's activities and vice versa. This implies cooperative monitoring, research, and study on an unprecedented scale. It implies a quite new readiness to take research wherever it is needed, with the backing of international financing. It means the fullest cooperation in converting knowledge into action.

Given our millennial habits of separate decision-making and the recent tremendous explosion of national power, how can any perception of the biosphere's essential unity and interdependence be combined with the separate sovereignty of more than 130 national governments? From family to clan, from clan to nation, from nation to federation – such enlargements of allegiance have occurred without wiping out the earlier loves. Today, in human society, we can perhaps hope to survive in all our prized diversity provided we can achieve an ultimate loyalty to our single, beautiful, and vulnerable planet Earth.

From: *Dialogue*, Vol. 6, No. 4, 1973

1.2. Lösungsweg und Lösungsvorschläge

I. Questions on the text
Read all the questions first, then answer them in the given order. Use your own words as far as it is appropriate.

Zweigeteilte Frage!

Antwort im 2. Absatz

1. **In what way was the prehistoric tribe the writer refers to in line 5 "the forerunner of the nation"? Why does he call its members "the world's first imperialists"?**

Der erste Teil dieser Frage zielt darauf ab, dass Sie die Gründe aufzählen, warum der Stamm vom Autor als *forerunner of the nation* bezeichnet wird, während der zweite Teil nach den Gründen fragt, warum der Autor die Stammesmitglieder als *first imperialists* bezeichnet. Die Antwort auf beide Teile finden Sie im 2. Absatz.

Stoffsammlung:
The prehistoric tribe was "the forerunner of the nation" because the members

- clustered around a fire
- had a language
- shared supernatural beliefs
- shared legends about their ancestors

The tribe members are called "the world's first imperialists" because they

- used phrases similar to "vital national interests" and "manifest destiny"
- massacred and enslaved weaker peoples who clustered around smaller fires

Formulierungshilfe:
The prehistoric tribe could be called "the forerunner of the nation" as it had a common place to live in, a common language, religion and history, features which, according to modern definition, are the constituents of a nation.
The author calls its members "the world's first imperialists" because, just like all imperialists, they subjugate smaller and weaker nations by killing their people or turning them into slaves. They justify this by claiming that it is their God-given right to put their own needs to the fore.

2. Which philosophical arguments prior to the 20th century provided the basis for the idea of a harmonious relationship between nations?

Antwort im vierten Absatz

Stoffsammlung:

Enlightenment: An ideology developed to govern the conduct of nations towards their own people: all human beings
- are born equal
- should enjoy certain basic liberties and rights
- should have the right to choose their leader

→ it was only reasonable to imagine a compact governing nations' behaviour towards one another.

Formulierungsvorschlag:

The philosophical arguments of the period of the Enlightenment provided the basis for the idea of a harmonious relationship between nations. Philosophers demanded that every individual should have the same basic rights because everybody was born equal. These rights included the right to decide on their own who should govern them. Thus they laid the foundation stones of democracy.

Once these principles had become commonly accepted, it was only logical that nations should then be able to regulate their relationships by means of contracts.

3. Outline the causes for the establishment of supranational organizations during the first half of the present century.

Antwort in den Absätzen 5 und 6

Stoffsammlung:

- the advent of electricity, radio and air travel
  - world becomes smaller
  - world's commercial life becomes less regulated
  - world's nations become more interdependent
  - world's conflicts become bloodier
- the price for leading wars becomes too high
- statesmen favoured giving primacy to supranational interests.

Formulierungshilfe:

With the invention of electricity, the growing importance of the media and freedom of movement, the world has become more interconnected and seems smaller to us. As a consequence, world trade has become easier, and thus countries have come to depend more on each other. At the same time wars have become more cruel and have claimed a greater number of lives than ever before. This is why politicians have come to understand that it is necessary to consider supranational interests more important than merely national ones.

Zweigeteilte Frage!

Antwort im 7. Absatz

4. What progress has been achieved on an economic level? Explain its national and global implications.

Achten Sie darauf, dass Sie es hier wieder mit einer zweigeteilten Frage zu tun haben: Zunächst müssen Sie den *progress* beschreiben und danach *its national and global implications* erklären. Beide Anworten finden Sie im 7. Absatz des Textes.

Stoffsammlung:
What progress has been achieved at an economic level?
- multilateral financial institutions
- International Monetary Fund, General Agreement on Tariffs and Trade

The national and global implications of the International Monetary Fund
- it dictates fiscal policies
  - how much tax should be levied on citizens?
  - how much can be charged on imports?
- National and global implications:
  - member states give up a degree of sovereignty
  - these organizations can be seen as protoministries of trade, finance and development

Formulierungshilfe:
At an economic level, supranational financial organizations such as the International Monetary Fund and the General Agreement on Tariffs and Trade, have been founded. These institutions have shifted the responsibility for tax and foreign trade politics from a national to an international level, limiting the sovereignty of individual states. To a certain extent they can be seen as future ministries which prepare nations for the unification of the world.

Antwort im 8. Absatz

5. What decisive changes took place in 1991?

Stoffsammlung:
- UN Security Council authorized allied troops to assist starving Kurds in northern Iraq.
- Since then the principle of "humanitarian intervention" has been gaining acceptance.

Formulierungshilfe:
Up to 1991 the world community did not interfere in national affairs. Then, however, UN troops were sent to northern Iraq to support the Kurds. From then on "humanitarian intervention", i.e. interference in internal affairs for the sake of humanitarian help, has become widely accepted.

6. What points does the writer try to prove by using Switzerland and Yu-goslavia as concrete examples? Antwort in Absatz 11

Stoffsammlung:
- differences need not divide
- to be in peaceful league with one another, people – and peoples – must have the benefits of democracy

Formulierungshilfe:
By mentioning Switzerland, of all countries, the author wants to prove that it is not impossible for different nationalities to live peacefully together. A pre-requisite for that is, however, according to the writer, the existence of a working democracy. This is why Yugoslavia failed in establishing a harmonious society in which its different ethnic groups could live together in peace.

7. What kind of reader is the article aimed at? Consider the structure and the style of the text.

Auch diese Frage ist zweigeteilt, da man zunächst die Struktur und den Stil des gesamten Textes analysieren muss um herauszufinden, auf welche Art von Leser der Text zugeschnitten ist.

Zweigeteilte Frage

Text muss als Ganzes analysiert werden

Stoffsammlung:
structure:
- an outline of the history of mankind, philosophy, politics and the "birth of
- the global nation"
- long, complex sentences and a sophisticated style of argumentation
style:
- the use of formal language written at the highest level
- a large number of hard words, i. e. words of Latin or Greek origin
- technical terms
- a great deal of history and philosophical theory
→ reader must have a sound general education to be able to understand the words and to follow the line of reasoning.

Formulierungsvorschlag:
The text "The Birth of the Global Nation" is a theoretical text which provides the reader with an outline of the history of mankind, philosophy, politics and of course the historical development of the world towards a global nation. The writer uses long sentences and complex lines of reasoning to make his point. These sentences consist of very formal language at a high linguistic level: A large number of hard words, for example "prehistoric" (l. 5), "proto-ministries" (ll. 46–47) or "environmental degradation" (l. 53), as well as technical terms such as "multilateral" (l. 41), "fiscal policies" (l. 43) or "levy taxes" (l. 44) are used. Furthermore, the text is full of history and philosophical theory. Taking all this into consideration it becomes evident that the reader needs not only to have a sound general education but also a vast vocabulary to be able to understand the text.

II. Composition

Choose one of the following topics.

1. Separatism versus world government. How do you explain these opposing trends?

Hier ist keine Bewertung der beiden Phänomene gefragt, sondern eine Erklärung ihrer Ursachen. Aus diesem Grund sollten die beiden Trends auch vom Umfang her in etwa gleich behandelt werden.

Formulierungsvorschlag zur Einleitung:

When following developments in world politics, different trends become visible. On the one hand organizations like the European Union and NATO are expanding towards what seems like a world government. On the other hand however, there are groups such as ETA that are desperately struggling for independence and moving towards separatism.
How can these opposing trends be explained?

**Tipp
siehe S. 12**

Lineares Thema mit zweiteiligem Hauptteil

Nicht die Bewertung der beiden Trends ist verlangt, sondern lediglich der Versuch einer Erklärung

Argumentationshilfen zur Erklärung des Trends "world government":

- With only one world government there will be no more wars between nations.
- A world government is the logical consequence of the growing importance of radio, TV and especially the internet which bring the world closer together.
- In times of progressive economic globalization why should one world be ruled by more than 130 different national governments?

Argumentationshilfen zur Erklärung des Trends "separatism":

- In a world in which differences between the nations become less and less important, people are afraid of losing their national identity (language, customs etc.).
- With the fall of frontiers, there is the danger of terrorism, diseases and crime spreading in an uncontrollable way.
- The taking of individual decisions is still seen as a demonstration of power by some national governments which do not want to have their power reduced.

Formulierungsvorschlag für den Schluss:

Paradoxical as they may seem, both trends, world government and separatism, have their origins in the growing globalization which has clearly been on the march in the last few decades. Whereas world government is one of its logical consequences, separatism is partially a reaction reflecting the fear of globalization.

2. "Nature knows no frontiers." Explain the topicality of this sentence with reference to environmental problems.

Achten Sie darauf, dass Sie nicht fälschlicherweise über Naturkatastrophen wie Erdbeben oder Vulkanausbrüche schreiben, da hier der Bezug zu der ausdrücklich in der Themenstellung geforderten Umweltproblematik fehlt!

Themenstellung nicht missverstehen!

Tipp
siehe S. 12

Lineares Thema

Formulierungsvorschlag für die Einleitung:

Nowadays it is frequently the case that countries try to "export" their environmental problems. For example many industrialized countries shift parts of their waste disposal to other countries, not only because of financial reasons but also to get rid of the dangers involved by banishing them beyond national frontiers. Nature itself, however, does not recognize any frontiers.

Argumentationshilfen:

- The explosion of a nuclear power plant at Chernobyl in 1986 showed clearly that, for example, nuclear radiation released by such a catastrophe does not stop at national borders.
- If the destruction of the ozone layer goes on, one day this will effect the whole world and not only those countries which are mainly responsible for the emission of CFCs.
- Even though it is mainly the industrialized countries that are responsible for the excessive emission of carbon dioxides, the consequences will probably first be felt by third world countries before they are felt by the whole world.

Formulierungshilfe für den Schluss:

These examples obviously show that national thinking does not lead anywhere when dealing with environmental problems. Catastrophes like Chernobyl, for example, can happen any day and anywhere, and both to prevent and to deal with them, a global consciousness is absolutely indispensable. We should follow the example given by nature itself and do away with frontiers.

3. Education for peace. What could be done in schools to further this idea?

Formulierungsvorschlag für die Einleitung:

Creating a peaceful world is one of the major challenges facing mankind in the 21st century. I firmly believe that this aim can only be achieved if we provide the younger generation with the means necessary to solve conflicts in a non-violent way. Apart from the upbringing in the family one of the first places where to start an education for peace is of course in schools.

Argumentationshilfen:

- As treating each other in a respectful way is the basis for living together in peace it is necessary for teachers to set an example when dealing with their pupils and to show them how to get on with each other, thus creating an atmosphere of mutual respect.
- Classes should not only be seen as a part of society but also as "small societies" in their own right in which the skills necessary to solve conflicts in a non-violent way are practised on a smaller scale.
- Education at schools could include projects where pupils of different nationalities learn about each other's cultural background.
- Some schools already have anti-conflict workgroups which mediate between pupils and help them to settle their conflicts. Such groups should be established in all schools.
- Exchange programmes provide an excellent opportunity to fight prejudices and to get to know other cultures.

Formulierungshilfe für den Schluss:

Of course I do not claim that these measures are enough to prevent wars between nations, especially as people's behaviour is not only influenced by schools, but also by their families, the media and their friends. Nevertheless I am convinced that, if schools began to take their responsibility in this area more seriously, a big step towards a more peaceful life could be made.

Viele Lehrkräfte legen großen Wert darauf, dass Fremdwörter, soweit möglich, ins Deutsche übertragen werden, um sicherzustellen, dass Sie auch die jeweilige Bedeutung verstanden haben. Die Übersetzung der vorliegenden Abituraufgabe enthält eine Fülle von Fremdwörtern. Da diese Ausdrücke Bestandteil der wissenschaftlichen Stilebene des Textes sind (schließlich könnte man auch im Englischen oft ein „englisches" Wort anstatt des Fremdwortes benutzen, z. B. „common" statt „collective"), wird in dieser Musterübersetzung häufig auf eine Übertragung verzichtet.

Wenn die Menschen sich bis jetzt nicht über das Ausmaß ihrer gegenseitigen Abhängigkeit auf diesem Planeten (1) bewusst geworden sind, dann war das zumindest teilweise darauf zurückzuführen, dass sie als klare, präzise, physikalische und wissenschaftliche Tatsache nicht existierte. Die neuen Einblicke in unsere Grundsituation/grundlegende Lebenssituation können auch zu Einblicken in unser Überleben werden.
Der erste Schritt zur Entwicklung einer Strategie für den Planeten Erde ist es, dass die Nationen (2) eine *kollektive* Verantwortung dafür übernehmen, viel mehr über das Ökosystem (3) herauszufinden und darüber, wie es durch menschliche Handlungen beeinflusst wird und umgekehrt. Das impliziert gemeinsames Beobachten, gemeinsame Forschung und gemeinsame Studien in noch nie da gewesenem Maßstab. Es impliziert eine ganz neue Bereitschaft, dort zu forschen, wo immer es notwendig ist, mit internationaler Finanzierung als Rückhalt. Es bedeutet die vollste Zusammenarbeit darin, Wissen in Taten umzusetzen.
Wie kann angesichts unserer jahrtausendealten Gewohnheit von eigener Entscheidungsfindung und der gewaltigen Explosion nationaler Macht in letzter Zeit irgendeine Wahrnehmung der grundsätzlichen Einheit und gegenseitiger Abhängigkeit unserer Biosphäre mit der getrennten Souveränität von mehr als 130 nationalen Regierungen in Einklang gebracht werden? Von der Familie zum Clan, vom Clan zur Nation, von der Nation zur Föderation/ zum Staatenbund – solche Erweiterungen der Loyalität haben stattgefunden, ohne die vorherigen engen Bindungen auszulöschen. Heute, in der menschlichen Gesellschaft, können wir vielleicht darauf hoffen, in all unserer wertvollen Vielfalt zu überleben, vorausgesetzt wir können eine ultimative Loyalität gegenüber unserem einzigartigen, wundervollen und verwundbaren Planeten Erde erreichen.

(1) *planetary* kann hier nicht mit „planetarisch" übersetzt werden, da das eine Abhängigkeit der Planeten untereinander implizieren würde.

(2) *nations* wird hier nicht mit „Länder" übersetzt, da es sich hier um die politische und nicht um die geografische Ebene handelt.

(3) Die wörtliche Übersetzung „natürliches System" oder „System der Natur" ergibt im Deutschen keinen Sinn.

2. Urban Problems

2.1. Text und Aufgaben

Zu bearbeitender Text

A Newsweek-NBC News poll shows that 88 percent of all Americans see their cities in negative terms and that 42 percent say crime and drugs are the most urgent urban problems. There is a sense of gloom and even helplessness at the dimensions of the urban dilemma – that dilemma is
5   race and poverty. And while the total number of poor people in the United States is actually declining, there is no question that America's larger cities are home to increasingly concentrated populations of people known as the unemployed poor.

What is striking about the urban-policy debate is the consensus that the
10 social problems of the cities and the underlying economic trends are now connected in a very dangerous way. The problem is what has been called a mismatch between workers' skills and job requirements. Experts maintain that the cities' gradual shift away from manufacturing has almost eliminated the blue-collar jobs traditionally occupied by the urban
15 poor – jobs that were the first step upward for millions of unskilled immigrants. The service-sector industries that have replaced manufacturing in the cities need employees who are able to work with words and numbers – while the urban poor, as a group, are very poorly educated. To make it worse, even these new jobs are beginning to move to the suburbs,
20 where they are practically out of reach for many city dwellers.

None of this means there are no answers to urban problems. City governments need to focus on the basics – public safety, adequate housing and education – to restore public confidence and hold their middle-class residents. To do that they need federal help in paying for the rising costs
25 of poverty. According to experts' poverty-related costs now consume at least 10 to 20 percent of the average city's budget. Since much of that money goes to provide health care for the poor and homeless, speedy action on a health-care reform would help the cities' finances.

One priority is probably the most crucial: making a long-term investment
30 in the children of the inner city. That means more federal money for infant nutrition and school-lunch programs and full funding for Head Start. It also means fundamental reform of the public schools, which is probably the best way to help poor children compete in the changing U.S. job market.

(Newsweek, September, 1991; 389 words)

12 *mismatch:* state of not fitting together well • 13 *manufacturing:* industrial production •
29 *crucial:* important • 31 *nutrition:* food • 31 *Head Start:* ein Vorschulprogramm

1. Vocabulary

In the following (items a–g) you are to deal with the underlined words/expressions within the given context.

a) 3: "… the most urgent urban problems."
Explain; you may change the sentence structure.

b) 6: "… is actually declining …"
Find suitable substitutes. Keep to the sentence structure.

c) 9: "What is striking about …"
Find suitable substitutes. Keep to the sentence structure.

d) 12–13: "Experts maintain that … "
Find suitable substitutes. Keep to the sentence structure.

e) 15–16: "… unskilled immigrants."
Explain; you may change the sentence structure.

f) 21–22: "City governments need to focus on …"
Explain; you may change the sentence structure.

g) 32: "… reform of the public schools, …"
Explain; you may change the sentence structure.

h) Find the corresponding *abstract nouns* (not the *-ing* forms):
  8: to know
16: to replace
23: to restore
27: to provide

2. Grammar and Style

a) 15–16: "… has almost eliminated the blue-collar jobs …"
Name the tense and explain its use.

b) 16: "… jobs traditionally occupied by the urban poor …"
Explain the construction and give an alternative.

c) 37: "… which is probably the best way …"
What does "which" refer to?

II. Comprehension

Answer the following questions in complete sentences.
Keep to the information given in the text, but do not quote.

1. What, according to the opening lines, are the symptoms of crisis in America's larger cities?

2. In what way are the social problems of the cities connected with economic trends?

3. What solutions to the problems are mentioned?

III. Comment

Choose one of the following topics.

1. What are the positive aspects of living in big cities such as New York and London?

2. The opening of the Channel Tunnel – a further step towards European integration?

IV. Translation

… The post-imperial world is more anarchic and perhaps even more dangerous than the imperial world used to be. The smaller powers are re-arming rapidly; it is only the major powers who are still disarming after the end of the Cold War. That will probably prove to be a short-term phase. There is likely to be a return to alliances which are chiefly concerned with security; Nato has been downgraded relative to the European Community, but that will probably reverse itself, as both Europe and America become aware of the complexity and danger of the post-imperial world.

In the meantime we have no strategy. The Cold War provided a world discipline. Everyone knew where the spheres of influence had been drawn; nations knew how far they could go. Now there is no sense of defined boundaries either of geography or of action; the Serbs have shown that it is possible, so far, to defy the world without intolerable consequences though the Serbian economy, like the Ukrainian, is an inflationary nightmare. The United States is the only power which could develop a new strategy. So far there has been no sign that President Clinton's Administration has either the will or the capacity to do so.

(*The Times*, 7 February, 1994; 202 words)

6 *to downgrade:* to make less important

Der Text dieses Zeitungsartikels wurde in der Originalprüfungsaufgabe leicht geändert. Wir bieten hier aber aus Copyrightgründen den Originalartikel.

2.2. Lösungsweg und Lösungsvorschläge

I. Language

Aufgaben zu Sprache und Stil

1. Vocabulary

a) 3: "… the <u>most urgent</u> urban problems."
Explain; you may change the sentence structure.

The urban problems <u>that need to be solved first</u>.

b) 6: "… is <u>actually declining</u> …"
Find suitable substitutes. Keep to the sentence structure.

… is <u>indeed decreasing</u>/<u>going down</u> …

c) 9: "What is <u>striking</u> about …"
Find suitable substitutes. Keep to the sentence structure.

What is <u>remarkable</u>/<u>noticeable</u> about …

d) 12–13: "Experts <u>maintain</u> that …"
Find suitable substitutes. Keep to the sentence structure.

Experts <u>claim</u> that …

e) 15–16: "… <u>unskilled</u> immigrants."
Explain; you may change the sentence structure.

… immigrants <u>without any professional training</u>.

f) 21–22: "City governments need to <u>focus</u> on …"
Explain; you may change the sentence structure.

City governments need to <u>concentrate</u> on …

g) 32: "… reform of the <u>public</u> schools …"
Explain; you may change the sentence structure.

… reform of the <u>state</u> schools …

h) Find the corresponding <u>abstract nouns</u> (not the –*ing* forms):

to know: knowledge
to replace: replacement
to restore: restoration
to provide: provision

2. Grammar and Style

a) 13–14: "… has almost eliminated the blue-collar jobs …"
Name the tense and explain its use.

The tense is called the present perfect. It is used to describe an action which has started in the past and is still going on.

b) 14–15: "… jobs traditionally occupied by the urban poor …"
Explain the construction and give an alternative.

The construction is a contact clause, i. e. a relative clause where the relative pronoun has been left out because it refers to the object. The alternative would be: "… jobs that/which have traditionally been occupied by the urban poor …"

c) 32–33: "… which is probably the best way …"
What does "which" refer to?

The "which" refers to the whole expression "fundamental reform of the public schools".

II. Comprehension

Aufgaben zum Textverständnis

Answer the following questions in complete sentences. Keep to the information given in the text, but do not quote.

1. What, according to the opening lines, are the symptoms of crisis in America's larger cities?

Antwort im ersten Absatz ("opening lines"!)

Stoffsammlung:
- crime and drugs
- the dilemma of race and poverty
- the increasing number of unemployed poor

Formulierungsvorschlag:
The opening lines say that the symptoms of crisis in America's larger cities are, above all, the problems related to drugs and crime. In addition to that there are race-related problems and the difficulties poor people face. Finally, America's bigger cities have to cope with ever higher numbers of jobless inhabitants who live below the poverty line.

2. In what way are the social problems of the cities connected with economic trends?

Antwort im zweiten Absatz

Stoffsammlung:
- a mismatch between workers' skills and job requirements
- the cities' shift away from manufacturing has eliminated blue-collar jobs
- manufacturing has been replaced by service-sector industries that need employees who are able to work with words and numbers
- even these new jobs have begun to move to the suburbs

Formulierungsvorschlag:
The social problems of the cities are connected with economic trends in an alarming way: Factory work and jobs for unskilled workers cannot be found in cities any longer while the service sector has grown and offers jobs that cannot be done by the workers with no professional training who live there. As a consequence the workers' abilities do not meet the demands of the job market. And, what is worse, even the jobs in the service sector are about to move away from the cities to the suburbs.

Antwort in den letzten beiden Absätzen

3. What solutions to the problems are mentioned?

Stoffsammlung
- city governments need to focus on public safety, adequate housing and education
- city governments need to restore public confidence and hold their middle-class residents
- federal help in paying for the rising costs of poverty is needed
- speedy action on a health care reform
- most crucial of all is the need to make a long-term investment in the children of the inner city → federal money for infant nutrition and school-lunch programmes, full funding for Head Start, fundamental reform of the public schools

Formulierungsvorschlag:
The text mentions various solutions to the problems in inner cities. It suggests that with federal financial help city governments would have the possibility to concentrate on protecting their citizens from drugs and crime, providing enough affordable flats and houses, and financing better schools. By taking these measures they could make sure that the better-off middle class inhabitants stay in the cities. Moreover, the health care system needs a thorough reform as too much money, which could be better spent elsewhere, is needed for the health care of poor citizens. Above all, it is necessary to invest great sums in food and education programmes for children.

III. Comment

Choose <u>one</u> of the following topics.

1. **What are the positive aspects of living in big cities such as New York and London?**

Tipp
siehe S. 12

Lineares Thema
(vgl. Teil A)

Formulierungsvorschlag zur Einleitung:
There is no denying the fact that crime, drugs and poverty are prevalent in almost every city of the Western world. Nevertheless there are still many people, especially the young, who would rather live in cities than in the country. What might be their possible reasons?

Argumentationshilfen:
- With universities to be found only in bigger cities, it is almost impossible to obtain a higher education in small towns or in the country.
- Many people enjoy the privacy brought about by the anonymity of big cities.
- People in cities have better possibilities to go shopping and enjoy a choice of a wider range of products, both in the food and in the non-food sectors.
- Cities offer a greater variety of cultural, social and spare time activities (theatres, concerts, cinemas, sports, discos, pubs etc.).
- As the job market is larger, it is often easier to find a job in the city.

Formulierungsvorschlag für den Schluss:
It is true that people living in cities have to cope with a great number of problems, but many of them are convinced that the positive aspects more than compensate for the negative ones.

Tipp
siehe S. 12

Meinungsthema
(vgl. Teil A)

2. The opening of the Channel Tunnel – a further step towards European integration?

Formulierungsvorschlag zur Einleitung:

When standing at Waterloo Station in London one can now see the Eurostar that bears a sign saying that this train is heading for Paris. The Channel Tunnel has finally brought Britain and the continent closer together. Can this be seen as a further step towards European integration?

Argumentationshilfen dafür:

- The transport of goods has become cheaper as unloading and boarding a ship is no longer necessary to cross the Channel.
- People also can reach England faster. They no longer have to use more than one means of transportation.

Argumentationshilfen dagegen:

- The planning of the Channel Tunnel was overshadowed by many discussions between France and Britain, concerning the language to be used for the signs in the tunnel and other matters.
- Britain will always be situated on the edge of Europe. No matter how good the connection to Europe, Britain will always be an island.
- Integration takes place mainly in the heads of the people, which means that neither tunnels nor bridges will further integration if people are not willing to integrate.

Formulierungsvorschläge für beide Schlussvarianten

dafür:
Considering all the pros and cons one must come to the conclusion that, no matter what opponents say, the Channel Tunnel was one of the most outstanding achievements in the history of European integration.

dagegen:
Taking everything into consideration one arrives at the conclusion that despite all the positive aims pursued with the construction of the Channel Tunnel, it is impossible to bring unwilling people together by means of tunnels.

Die post-imperiale (1) Welt ist anarchistischer und vielleicht sogar gefährlicher als zuvor geworden. Die kleineren Mächte bewaffnen sich rasch aufs Neue; es sind nur die Hauptmächte, die nach dem Ende des Kalten Krieges noch immer abrüsten. Dies wird sich wahrscheinlich als eine kurz andauernde Phase herausstellen. Eine Rückkehr zu den Bündnissen, denen die Sicherheit ein Hauptanliegen ist, ist wahrscheinlich; die NATO wurde im Vergleich zur Europäischen Union degradiert, aber das wird sich wahrscheinlich ins Gegenteil kehren, in dem Maße, da sich sowohl Europa als auch Amerika der Komplexität und der Gefährlichkeit der post-imperialen Welt bewusst werden.

In der Zwischenzeit haben wir keine Strategie. Der Kalte Krieg hat für weltweite Disziplin gesorgt. Jeder wusste, wo die Grenzen (2) der Einflussbereiche gezogen waren; die Nationen wussten, wie weit sie gehen konnten. Jetzt gibt es kein Bewusstsein für definierte Grenzen, weder in Bezug auf die Geografie noch in Bezug auf Taten; die Serben haben gezeigt, dass es bisher möglich ist, der Welt ohne unerträgliche Konsequenzen zu trotzen, obwohl die serbische Wirtschaft wie die ukrainische ein inflationärer Albtraum ist. Die Vereinigten Staaten sind die einzige Macht, die eine Strategie entwickeln könnte. Bis jetzt gibt es kein Anzeichen, dass Präsident Clintons Regierung den Willen oder die Fähigkeit hat das zu tun.

(1) Das bedeutet hier nach dem Zerfall der Sowjetunion als der größten Weltmacht.

(2) Zur Sinnergänzung wurde hier das Wort „Grenzen" eingefügt.

3. The Reluctant Father

3.1. Text und Aufgaben

Zu bearbeitender Text

Robert Razowsky, 32, changes diapers, bathes his son and gets up for night feedings. He once dutifully went to a Dad's Sunday at his son's Moms and Tots class. But the gas-station owner from suburban Chicago is more likely to be found at a Bears game on weekends, and he suspects
5 that a lot of his friends would also rather go to a ball game than bond with their kids. "If I had to take care of children 50-50, would I still want them?" he asks. "I don't know."

Most fathers have become reluctant warriors in a social revolution. Now that even the most traditional women are going off to work, the pressure
10 is on dad to help more – if not share equally – on the home front. He is supposed to be the new sensitive man, caring and warm. Yet most men were raised to succeed at work, not at home. When his role as breadwinner is undermined, often his ego is too. A father may not think he's very good at child rearing; lacking a proper role model, he may be right.

15 Is Mr. Mom a myth? Yes, says Glen Palm, professor of child and family studies at St. Cloud State University in Minnesota. "We've been wanting to put men on an equal plane too quickly. There are very, very few men who belong there." Most men know they ought to do more to raise their children, but that doesn't mean they really want to. If it's hard for the
20 new woman to "have it all," it's just as hard for the new man to be the close, caring father his own father probably never was.

Men do pitch in at home more than their fathers did, but still not nearly as much as their wives. Most studies show that women do two or three times as much housework and child rearing as their husbands.

25 Government and business are slowly moving to make it easier for men to share the load. Even the macho Los Angeles Fire Department now permits men to bring babies to the fire station. Six states have passed laws requiring employers to give both mother and father time off when they have a new baby or seriously ill child. Congress narrowly failed to pass a
30 similar bill this fall; the legislation is expected to pass next year.

But will men take the time off when it's offered? Some companies do report an increase in male employees requesting benefits that will allow them to spend more time with their children. Still, men who stay at home for more than a week or so are in the minority.

35 Part of men's intransigence is purely economic: men on average still make more money than women. "Typically the father gets put to work because that's where his time can be most efficiently spent," says Professor Palm. "Until women's pay is equal to men's, they won't have an equal opportunity to develop parenting skills."

40 Still, there's no substitute for the kind of parenting a father can provide. Studies indicate that babies are more aware of their fathers than previously thought. Fathers tend to be more playful and physical than mothers. They encourage their children to be more persistent at tasks and to take more risks. And while highly masculine fathers don't necessarily
45 raise highly masculine sons, research now suggests that girls whose fathers encouraged them to be athletic and competitive are more likely to be high achievers in later life.

From: *Newsweek*, January 2, 1989

3 *Moms and Tots class:* group for mothers and small children • 4 *The Chicago Bears:* American football team • 5–6 *bond with:* form a close relationship with • 22 *pitch in:* add one's help or support • 35 *intransigence:* unwillingness to change one's attitude

I. Questions on the text

Read all the questions first, then answer them in the given order. Use your words as far as is appropriate.

1. What changes in the understanding of male and female roles characterize the social revolution mentioned in the text? To what extent does Robert Razowsky live up to the expectations of this revolution?

2. What are the obstacles that stand in the way of this social revolution?

3. What progress has been made outside the home in response to the changing situation?

4. How do recent scientific studies view the father's role in child care?

5. What means does the writer employ to make his article appear objective? Give evidence.

II. Composition

Choose o n e of the following topics.

1. "The hand that rocks the cradle rules the world." Discuss this proverb.

2. Some people say that our society has a negative attitude towards children. What is your opinion?

III. Translation

Translate the following text into German:

In the past, discussion about working wives tended to centre on the conflict between women's two roles – as housewives and mothers, and as workers outside the home. The scope of this discussion is now being enlarged to encompass the two roles of men, and the conflict between the demands of the world of work and the demands of family life. Prejudice and confusion remain, however, in judgements of married women's status. The expectation that women will be primarily responsible for the therapeutic and caring roles in the family creates considerable difficulties for married women wanting to return to work. While many of the legal and political barriers to equal status between men and women have been removed and, since 1945, many of the restrictions on the employment of married women have similarly disappeared, other barriers remain. These involve deep-rooted attitudes, ideals and expectations held not only among husbands and wives but also among employers and co-workers.

From: J. Ryder, H. Silver, *Modern English Society* (1977)

3.2. Lösungsweg und Lösungsvorschläge

I. Questions on the text

Answer the following questions in complete sentences. Keep to the information given in the text, but do not quote.

1. **What changes in the understanding of male and female roles characterize the social revolution mentioned in the text? To what extent does Robert Razowsky live up to the expectations of this revolution?**

Zweigeteilte Frage

Antwort im 1. und 2. Absatz

Zweigeteilte Frage: Zunächst müssen die *changes* in der männlichen und weiblichen Rolle dargestellt werden, um danach die Rolle von R. R. im Rahmen dieser *social revolution* zu beschreiben. Die Antworten finden Sie im ersten und zweiten Absatz.

Stoffsammlung:
changes
- even the most traditional women are going off to work
- there is pressure on dad to work more at home
- man is supposed to be sensitive, caring and warm
- his role as breadwinner is undermined → his ego, too

Robert Razowsky
- changes diapers
- gets up for night feedings
- once dutifully went to Dad's Sunday at his son's Moms and Tots class
- he doesn't do all this voluntarily but rather because he is expected to do so

Formulierungsvorschlag:
The most striking change in the understanding of male and female roles that characterizes the "social revolution" is the fact that more and more women are deciding not only to care for their families but to work outside the home as well. As a consequence men are forced to support their wives in what was formerly considered women's work. The "new man" is expected to be emotional and affectionate towards his wife and children. Challenging man's traditional role as the sole provider, this new role reduces his self-confidence. Robert Razowsky is the best example of the "new man": He cares for his baby by changing nappies, getting up in the middle of the night to feed him and by showing interest in all his son's concerns. However, he does not do all this totally voluntarily, but rather because his wife expects him to do so.

Antwort: 2., 3. und
7. Absatz

2. What are the obstacles that stand in the way of this social revolution?

Stoffsammlung:
- Lacking a proper role model a father may not be very good at child rearing.
- Society has been wanting to put men on an equal plane too quickly.
- Most men do not really want to do more to raise their children.
- It's just as hard for the man to be the close, caring father as it is for the women to do both, work and have a family.
- As men's pay is usually higher than women's, it is logical that it's mostly the women who stay at home.

Formulierungsvorschlag:
There are internal as well as external obstacles that stand in the way of the social revolution described in the text. Even if most men are aware of the fact that they should spend more time caring for their children, they are not really keen on doing so. The role of the affectionate father is too recent to have been shown to them by their own fathers. This is partly due to the fact that there has been too little time to prepare men properly for their new emancipated role society expects of them. Moreover, fulfilling the expectations of both roles, that of simultaneous father and breadwinner, is as difficult for men as it is for women. The traditional male and female roles are furthermore consolidated by the fact that men generally earn more than women, which makes it seem more sensible for the women to be the ones who stay at home full-time with their children.

Antwort in Absatz 5

3. What progress has been made outside the home in response to the changing situation?

Stoffsammlung:
- In six states there is a law that gives fathers and mothers time off when they have a new baby or a seriously ill child.
- This is expected to become federal law soon.
- LA Fire Dept. permits men to bring babies to work.

Formulierungsvorschlag:
Business and government have responded in a positive way to the changing situation. New laws in six states make it possible for both men and women to stay at home when they have a new-born baby or when their children are seriously ill. This will probably become federal law soon. Many firms and institutions even allow their employees to come to work with their babies, even the "macho Los Angeles Fire Department" (l. 26).

4. How do recent scientific studies view the father's role in child care? Antwort im letzten Absatz

Stoffsammlung:
- There is no substitute for the kind of parenting a father can provide.
- Babies are more aware of their father than previously thought.
- Fathers tend to be more playful and physical than mothers.
- Fathers encourage children to be more persistent at tasks and to take more risks.
- Highly masculine fathers don't necessarily raise highly masculine sons.
- Girls whose fathers encouraged them to be athletic are more likely to be high achievers in later life.

Formulierungshilfe:
Recent scientific studies show that fathers are much more important for their sons and daughters than they were considered to be. They play more with their children than mothers do and in a different way, and they tell their children to be more courageous and not to give up too soon. Whereas girls who were encouraged by their fathers to do sports tend to be more successful in their lives, sons of very masculine fathers are not always very masculine themselves.

5. What means does the writer employ to make his article appear objective?

Zur Beantwortung dieser Frage müssen Sie den gesamten Text auf Hinweise durchsuchen und analysieren. Analyse des gesamten Textes

Stoffsammlung:
- refers to scientific studies
- quotes scientists
- doesn't use any expressions that show his personal attitude
- uses quotations from interviews

Formulierungshilfe:
As a writer for the news magazine Newsweek the author should make his article appear as objective as possible. He achieves this aim by making use of several means: Firstly, he uses quotations from interviews to support his own theory. He is furthermore careful not to use any expressions that would show his personal attitude towards the subject, such as "I think" or "In my opinion", but sticks to mere facts instead. Apart from that he quotes a scientist and refers to scientific studies to get his point across.

Tipp
siehe S. 13

Dialektisches Thema

II. Comment

Choose o n e of the following topics.

1. "The hand that rocks the cradle rules the world." Discuss this proverb.

Formulierungsvorschlag zur Einleitung:
"The hand that rocks the cradle rules the world" – This proverb implies that those who educate and bring up children have an enormous influence on the future behaviour and personality of the children they are responsible for. As children are usually considered to be the future of the world, it follows that the way in which children are brought up shapes the world of the future. But is it really a simple matter to shape people according to one's wishes?

Argumentationshilfen dafür:
- Even though it has not been scientifically proven, recent studies suggest that children's intelligence is to a certain extent influenced by the environment in which they are brought up.
- Totalitarian regimes have always tried to gain control over the education of the children in their countries in order to "breed" loyal citizens.
- People tend to treat others in the same way they were treated in their childhood. Statistics, for example, show that children who experienced violence as a means of education are much more likely to use violence themselves in their later lives.

Argumente dagegen:
- Children are not only influenced by their parents, they are subject to other influences as well (e. g. friends, school, extended family).
- By means of education one cannot make sure that children behave in a certain way, because especially in their puberty children tend to do exactly the opposite of what they are expected to.
- As the example of East Germany shows, education in pursuit of a certain ideology no longer works when conditions change: Many youths from East Germany who were educated as good communist citizens, turned to the extreme right after German reunification.

Formulierungsvorschlag für beide Schlussvarianten:

dafür:
Taking everything into consideration it is obvious that the way in which children are brought up has an undeniable influence on their future behaviour. Of course education and upbringing are not the only factors that shape a child's personality, but they play a pivotal role.

dagegen:
It is true that a person's upbringing has a strong influence on his or her personality. That, however, does not mean that children can be conditioned for a certain purpose. Every kind of education, especially when it is based on ideology, may have the opposite effect to the one desired.

2. Some people say that our society has a negative attitude towards children. What is your opinion?

Formulierungsvorschlag zur Einleitung:
When looking at other countries we can see that there are cultures in which children are regarded as one of the most precious goods one can have. In most Western countries, however, it seems as though our society almost has a negative attitude towards children.

Argumentationshilfen dafür:
- Having children involves the danger of having to live below the poverty line as families need more money while at the same time it is difficult for both parents to work full-time.
- It is hard for families to find proper and affordable housing.
- Important political decisions are often taken without taking children's needs into consideration.

Argumentationshilfen dagegen:
- In our modern society children grow up with less restrictions than they did a few generations ago.
- The state provides different kinds of financial support for families.
- In many towns activities for children such as children's theatres, sports events or Moms and Tots groups are offered.

Formulierungsvorschläge für beide Schlussvarianten:

dafür:
With the exception of some positive-minded people, society has little regard for children and does not encourage young adults to start a family.

dagegen:
In conclusion I should like to say that even if families do face manifold problems in our society, one cannot claim that the society as a whole has a negative attitude towards children.

Tipp
siehe S. 12

Meinungsthema

III. Translation

In der Vergangenheit konzentrierte sich die Diskussion über berufstätige Ehefrauen zumeist auf den Konflikt zwischen den beiden Rollen der Frau (1) – als Hausfrau und Mutter einerseits (2), und als Berufstätige (3) außerhalb des Hauses andererseits. Der Umfang dieser Diskussion wird gerade erweitert und umfasst nun die beiden Rollen des Mannes (1) und den Konflikt zwischen den Anforderungen der Arbeitswelt und den Anforderungen des Familienlebens. Vorurteile und Verwirrung bleiben jedoch in der Beurteilung der Stellung verheirateter Frauen bestehen. Die Erwartung, dass die Frau hauptsächlich für die therapeutische und sorgende Rolle in der Familie verantwortlich/zuständig ist (4), schafft erhebliche Schwierigkeiten für verheiratete Frauen, die in den Beruf zurückkehren wollen. Während viele der rechtlichen (5) und politischen Hindernisse, die einer gleichberechtigten Stellung von Mann und Frau im Wege standen (6) beseitigt wurden, und während seit 1945 auch viele der Einschränkungen bei der Beschäftigung verheirateter Frauen in ähnlicher Weise verschwunden sind, bleiben andere Hindernisse auch weiterhin bestehen. Diese umfassen tief verwurzelte Einstellungen, Ideale und Erwartungen, die nicht nur von Ehemännern und Ehefrauen gehegt werden, sondern auch von Arbeitgebern und Mitarbeitern.

(1) Im Deutschen ist es üblicher, den Singular zu benutzen, wenn man über eine Sache oder Personengruppe im Allgemeinen spricht.

(2) Um den Konflikt zwischen den beiden Rollen auch sprachlich hervorzuheben, benutzen wir die Formulierung mit „einerseits …, andererseits …".

(3) "Arbeiterin" beschränkt sich im Deutschen häufig auf ungelernte Arbeitskräfte.

(4) Das englische *will* kann im Deutschen auch eine allgemein gültige Wahrheit ausdrücken und wird dann mit dem Präsens übersetzt.

(5) *legal* kann hier nicht mit "legal" übersetzt werden, da es um die Gesetzgebung geht und nicht um kriminelle Machenschaften.

(6) *barriers to* kann im Deutschen nur unzureichend mit einer entsprechenden Präposition wiedergegeben werden. Deswegen wurde hier ein gleichbedeutendes Verb eingefügt.

4. Slave Weavers

4.1. Text und Aufgaben

A child's pain is knotted deep into the designs of many Indian hand-woven carpets. Take, for instance, the case of the Queen's new carpet. Now decorating a hall at Windsor Castle, this richly patterned carpet was bought by her more than a year ago in London. It was woven by dozens
5 of Indian children, some as young as seven, who had been sold by their parents to loom owners as bonded labourers. The carpet was originally bought for more than £ 17,000 and reportedly resold to the Queen for £ 47,000.

The child weavers, who spent months tying each tiny knot of the carpet
10 individually on the harp-like strings of the loom, were lucky to get a meal and a few rupees a day. The children are supposed to be paid for each knot, but often the money is pocketed by the loom owner

Askari Imam, an official of the Children's Emancipation Society in New Delhi, which estimates the number of child weavers in India at more than
15 150,000, said: "It's like a slave's bazaar. There are touts who go to Bihar – it's one of the most impoverished spots of the world – and they buy these children to work in the looms. After the tenth or eleventh child, there's little emotional attachment that the parents feel towards the child."

The parents also know that however miserable a life at the looms may be
20 for their son or daughter, it will at least save them from dying of starvation. "Some of these children are bonded labourers for life. And their life is very short. If they try to escape they are caught and beaten," said Mr Imam.

Britain is the third biggest buyer of India's hand-woven carpets. The
25 main buyers of India's $ 250 million carpet exports are the United States and Germany, but both countries will soon pass tough new laws on goods made by child labour. A US bill will ban products made abroad by children. Imports to the US will require certificates, endorsed by human rights groups, proving that child labour is not used. The Americans want
30 fines imposed on law breakers but the German idea is to give the consumer a choice: handmade goods from India and other developing countries which are not crafted by children will bear a sticker saying so. A total ban, the Germans say, would make thousands of Indian families even poorer.

Zu bearbeitender Text

35 "This will be a major setback for the Indian carpet-makers," said Mr Imam. India has laws banning child labour but they are seldom enforced. As a start, the New Delhi government is registering all looms around Mirzapur to find out how many children are toiling in the industry.

Although Britain is not yet considering legislation similar to the US and
40 Germany's some British businessmen have been at the forefront of improving the plight of the child weavers.

Now Britain, the European Community and the International Labour Organisation are expanding programmes to help the children. Some human rights activists in the Mirzapur area have prodded the police into raiding
45 the looms and freeing the children. But, once they are returned to their homes, parents who cannot feed them invariably sell them back to the loom owners.

The tack taken by the Children's Emancipation Society has been to set up schools near the looms so the children can study in the mornings and
50 weave in the afternoons.

"We give them a meal, 100 rupees (£ 1.90) a month, some vocational training, and a little time for sports. Otherwise, these boys and girls are having to weave away their childhoods," said Mr Imam, adding: "After a little education, these children are starting to assert their rights. They're
55 demanding at least 30 rupees (60p) a day for weaving."

From: Tim McGirk, *The Independent*, January 2, 1993 (shortened)

38 *Mirzapur:* town in northern India • 48 *tack:* (hier) policy

I. Language/Form

1. Paraphrase the underlined word: "… but often the money is <u>pocketed</u> by the loom owner." (line 12)

2. This article is taken from a quality newspaper. Name two typical features of the "qualities" and give corresponding examples from the text.

II. Comprehension
(Use your own words as far as possible.)

1. Describe the situation of the child weavers.

2. What makes Indian parents sell their children?

3. Point out all the measures planned and undertaken to improve the children's plight.

III. Comment
(Choose one of the following topics.)

1. What can and must be done to help the children of the Third World? Express your ideas.

2. A happy childhood is a precondition to being successful as a grown-up. Discuss this statement.

3. Is it right to bring children into this world? Give your personal opinion.

IV. Translation
Translate lines 24–38 (from: "Britain is …" up to "… in the industry.").

4.2. Lösungsweg und Lösungsvorschläge

Aufgaben zu Sprache und Stil

I. Language/Form

1. Paraphrase the underlined word: "… but often the money is <u>pocketed</u> by the loom owner." (line 12)

… but often the money is taken/kept dishonestly by the loom owner.

Fundstellen genau belegen (vgl. Teil A)

2. This article is taken from a quality newspaper. Name two typical features of the qualities and give corresponding examples from the text.

Hier ist neben einer Untersuchung des Textes auch landeskundliches Hintergrundwissen über die britische Zeitungslandschaft gefragt. Ihre Belegstellen müssen Sie genau zitieren (vgl. Teil A).

Stoffsammlung:
content
- information of a purely factual nature; rumours are clearly distinguished from facts:
  - the Queen's new carpet (ll. 2–8)
  - Britain as the third biggest buyer of India's hand-woven carpets (l. 20)
- background information
  - legislation in the US and Germany (ll. 25–27)
  - a statement by the Children's Emancipation Society (e. g. ll. 15–18)
language
- elaborate, formal language
  - long sentences
  - hard words: emotional attachment (l. 18); endorsed (l. 28); expanding (l. 43);
  - creative use of language: "A child's pain is knotted deep into the […] carpets" (ll. 1–2); "having to weave away their childhoods" (l. 53)
  - personal opinion or emotions are not disclosed

Formulierungsvorschlag:
In contrast to tabloid papers, quality newspapers like "The Independent" stick to the facts as far as possible. In this article, for example, the reader is presented with information concerning the Queen's new carpet from India (ll. 2–8). The part of it which cannot be verified is clearly indicated as a rumour by means of the word "reportedly". (l. 7) The facts are supported by background information and presented in formal and elaborate language, which is another important feature of quality newspapers. The sentence structure is quite complex and use is made of rather sophisticated words such as "emotional attachment" (l. 18); "endorsed" (l. 28) "expanding" (l. 43). Moreover, quality papers often make creative use of language, which implies an educated readership. The expression "A child's pain is knotted deep into the […] carpets" (ll. 1–2), for example, uses the verb "to knot" in allusion to the work the children do.

II. Comprehension

Use your own words as far as possible.

1. Describe the situation of the child weavers.

Antwort in den Absätzen 2, 3, 4, 8

Stoffsammlung:

There are more than 150,000 child weavers, who
- are very young; some are only seven years old
- are sold by their parents as bonded labourers
- are lucky to get a meal and a few rupees a day, even if they are supposed to be paid for each knot
- are sometimes forced to remain as bonded labourers for life
- are caught and beaten if they try to escape
- are often resold when brought back to their parents

Formulierungsvorschlag:

The situation of the child weavers in India is desperate. There are more than 150,000 of them, most of them sold to carpet makers by their parents and treated like slaves throughout their whole life. Some of them are only seven years old and most of them do not get proper pay. When they run away from the looms, they are often brought back and mistreated. Sometimes human rights activists bring back some of them to their parents, who, lacking the money to feed them, resell them.

2. What makes Indian parents sell their children?

Antwort in den Absätzen 3 und 4

Stoffsammlung:
- Many parents cannot afford to raise their children.
- After the tenth or eleventh child, the parents have little emotional attachment to the child.
- The parents know that selling a child would at least save them from dying of starvation.

Formulierungsvorschlag:

The main reason that makes some Indian parents sell their children to carpet makers is that they live in incredible poverty. They cannot even afford to buy food for their children and hope that the carpet makers will at least feed them and thus save them from dying of hunger. For this very reason they have no other choice but to resell them when they are freed by the police and brought back home. And, in addition to that, some Indian parents are not capable of having a loving and caring relationship with each of their many children.

3. Point out all the measures planned and undertaken to improve the children's plight.

Stoffsammlung:
planned:
- A US bill will ban products made by children abroad.
- Imports to the US will require certificates proving that child labour has not been used in their manufacture.
- In Germany, hand-made goods from India not made by children will bear a sticker saying so.

undertaken:
- India has laws banning child labour (which are seldom enforced).
- All looms will be registered to find out how many children work there.
- Sometimes police raid the looms, free the children and return them to their homes.
- The Children's Emancipation Society has set up schools near the looms, where child weavers are given a meal, some money, vocational training and a little time for sports. → children discover their rights.

Formulierungsvorschlag:
The most important buyers, the US and Germany, are about to pass stricter laws concerning the import of Indian carpets: In the US, the import of carpets woven by children will be prohibited. Handmade products will need a document proving that child labour was not involved. These laws will be strictly enforced. In Germany, on the other hand, it is thought that prohibiting the import totally would increase poverty in India. The decision to purchase carpets labelled as having been produced without child labour will be left to the customer. India itself does already have laws that forbid child labour. Controls, however are rare.

There are other measures to improve the plight of Indian children that have already been taken: The New Delhi government has begun to register all looms to find out how many children are working there. Furthermore, police raids on looms have been carried out to free the children working there.

Finally, the Children's Emancipation Society has opened schools in the vicinity of the looms to make it possible for the young workers to go to school in the mornings and work for the rest of the day. There they are fed, get the opportunity to do sports and are given some money as well as professional training. Consequently, they become aware of their rights and, after a certain period of time, have the courage to demand proper payment for their work.

III. Comment

Choose one of the following topics.

1. What can and must be done to help the children of the Third World? Express your ideas.

Tipp siehe S. 101

Lineares Thema

Formulierungsvorschlag zur Einleitung:
Not only in India, but also in other Third World countries children have to lead a miserable life full of hardship. In a globalized world it ought to be the moral duty of every nation to help the countries affected to do something about this situation and thus improve the dismal lives of these children.

Argumentationshilfen:
- Industrialized countries should control the import of hand made products.
- Proper health care should be provided to reduce the infant mortality rate.
- Birth control has to be promoted, because it is easier for parents to provide for fewer children.
- Educational work has to be done to make people see the importance of education for their children.
- Schools have to be established everywhere and at no expense to the parents.
- Fair wages should be given to all workers so that they no longer depend on their children to contribute to the family income.

Formulierungsvorschlag für den Schluss:
Although there is no shortage of ideas as to how best to alleviate child poverty and exploitation in the Third World, little will be achieved unless people in industrialized countries, that is we ourselves, are prepared to pay fair prices for Third World products instead of wanting to save money wherever possible. Fair trade is the beginning of a fair chance for all.

**Tipp
siehe S. 13**

Dialektisches Thema

2. A happy childhood is a precondition to being successful as a grown-up. Discuss the statement.

Formulierungsvorschlag zur Einleitung:

A difficult childhood is often used as an excuse for the many predicaments and evils people encounter as adults, such as failure, violence, drugs and so on. On the other hand people also like to point out that a happy childhood is an important key to success as a grown up. Is childhood really that important?

Argumentationshilfen dafür:

- Happy children do not have to cope with too many conflicts and serious difficulties and thus have more time to develop and cultivate their own interests and ambitions.
- Unhappy children often lack the self-confidence necessary for a successful life.
- Psychological studies show that people with a happy childhood are more likely to become balanced adults.

Argumentationshilfen dagegen:

- Why of all qualities should happiness be the gauge of success?
- People who are mentally strong can also cope with an unhappy childhood and become successful grown ups.
- Childhood cannot be made responsible for everything one does or achieves in later life.
- Having to cope with serious conflicts in childhood makes children more mature and ready to manage difficulties in their future life.

Formulierungsvorschläge für beide Schlussvarianten:

dafür:

In conclusion one has to admit that, even if childhood cannot be held responsible for everything in people's lives, it is a key factor in their psychological development and thus helps to pave their way for a successful life, if success is taken to mean living a satisfactory and happy life.

dagegen:

After weighing up all the pros and cons it cannot be denied that childhood plays an important role in people's lives, but a happy childhood is by no means a precondition for a successful life as there are enough people who are successful in spite of an unhappy childhood.

3. Is it right to bring children into this world? Give your personal opinion.

Tipp
siehe S. 12

Meinungsthema

Formulierungsvorschlag zur Einleitung:
Ever since the introduction of reliable means of contraception people have started to ask themselves if they really want to start a family. Apart from personal reasons they have often pondered whether it is right to bring children into this world or not.

Argumentationshilfen dafür:
- Without children the human race would soon die out.
- We all need somebody to care for us once we are old and need help and care ourselves.
- New generations bring forth new hopes, ideas and solutions for the problems of the world.

Argumentationshilfen dagegen:
- Parents cannot guarantee their children a good education or a happy and successful life.
- Today's world is already overpopulated and more children contribute to more problems such as a scarcity of food, pollution of the environment and a lack of natural resources.
- When one considers problems such as pollution, wars and violence, it is irresponsible to bring children into this world.

Formulierungsvorschläge für beide Schlussvarianten:

dafür:
Of course nobody in his right mind can hope to eliminate all the risks involved in bringing up and educating children, but, as reproduction is the basis for the existence of the human race, no one should deny themselves the wish to have children. The decision to have a family should be based on personal reasons not on man's general needs.

dagegen:
After careful consideration I have come to the conclusion that, even if there are good reasons for starting a family, the fact remains that this is no longer everybody's personal decision. After all, children brought into this world do not only affect their parents' lives but also the whole global society. With an ever growing population worsening the world's environmental and social problems, it becomes more and more irresponsible to give birth to children.

Großbritannien ist der drittgrößte Abnehmer von handgewebten Teppichen aus Indien. Die Hauptabnehmer der Teppichexporte Indiens im Wert von 250 Millionen Dollar sind die Vereinigten Staaten und Deutschland, aber beide Länder werden bald strenge neue Gesetze verabschieden, die Waren, welche in Kinderarbeit hergestellt werden (1), betreffen. Eine amerikanische Gesetzesvorlage wird Produkte verbieten, die im Ausland von Kindern hergestellt werden (1). Für Einfuhren in die Vereinigten Staaten werden von Menschenrechtsorganisationen bestätigte Bescheinigungen verlangt werden, die beweisen, dass keine Kinderarbeit verwendet wird. Die Amerikaner wollen, dass Gesetzesbrecher mit Geldstrafen belegt werden; die Absicht in Deutschland hingegen besteht darin, dem Verbraucher eine Wahl zu lassen: handgefertigte Waren aus Indien und anderen Entwicklungsländern, die nicht von Kindern hergestellt wurden, werden einen Aufkleber tragen, der eben das bestätigt. Ein völliges Verbot, sagen die Deutschen, würde tausende indischer Familien noch ärmer machen.

„Dies wird ein schwerer Rückschlag für die indischen Teppichhersteller", sagt Mr. Imam. Indien hat Gesetze, die Kinderarbeit verbieten, aber sie werden selten durchgesetzt. Um einen Anfang zu machen, registriert die Regierung in Neu Delhi gerade alle Webereien in der Umgebung von Mirzapur, um herauszufinden, wie viele Kinder sich in dieser Industrie abmühen/plagen.

(1) Hier ist auch eine Vergangenheitsform (*wurden/worden sind*) möglich, weil das englische Partizip sich auf keine Zeit festlegt und der Kontext hier mehrere Interpretationen zulässt.

5. Angry Young Men

5.1. Text und Aufgaben

Young, working-class, unemployed males are in crisis, yet few politicians or social scientists dare speak out about the gathering problem posed by a marginalised generation failing socially and economically and with no prospect of bettering itself.

Zu bearbeitender Text

5 Dr John Habgood, the Archbishop of York, recently linked the breakdown of marriage to women's emancipation and the rising number of young men regarded as simply not worth marrying. Young, unskilled men, once the backbone of industry, are becoming increasingly redundant now that neither employers nor women appear to have any use for
10 them.

Some of their resentment manifests itself in anti-social behaviour that only marginalises them still further: from venomous football crowds to illiterate scroungers, who, still in their teens, have fathered three or four illegitimate children.

15 Helped by a fundamental change in working patterns, women have seized their chance. Two out of three women now work, 60% of them full-time; by the year 2000, more women will be working than men. Over the next five years, according to figures prepared for the Equal Opportunities Commission, another 300,000 traditionally "male" jobs – in engi-
20 neering, building and manufacturing – will be lost, while 500,000 new "female" jobs in service industries and information technology – will be created.

As the economy shifts towards more part-time working, virtually no unskilled young man can expect to play the traditional role of breadwinner.
25 Women are increasingly prepared to get by without them In January, for example, there were 127,000 men aged 18–24 who had been unemployed for more than a year, compared with only 38,000 women.

"Young males have no role in society," says Clare Short, Labour's spokesman on women's issues. "They can't get stable incomes, so they
30 are useless partners or fathers. If your society can't give you a role, or respect, you despise it. Boys of 15 or 16 get into a drop-out culture of the streets; they are sullen and rude. It is a very murky world and it leads to getting money illegitimately. You can see the potential disaster. We are storing up a social crisis."

35 Ladywood, her Birmingham constituency, was once a centre of engineering and manufacturing. In the recession of the early 1980s, unemployment rose from 9 % to 40 %. The local economy has begun to pick up, but the new jobs – often in service industries – are usually alien to young men leaving school without skills. Until men learn to be more flexible, to swal-
40 low their contempt for such "soft" jobs, their prospects will remain grim.

Until recently, the convention had been that girls were ahead until their early teens, before starting to fall back because of the onset of puberty and the lower expectations of parents and teachers. That has all been swept aside. Girls are now outperforming boys in all subjects. In 1993,
45 45.8 % of girls achieved five GCSES at grades A, B or C. Only 36.8 % of boys could boast the same. Girls are twice as likely as boys to get an A grade at English A-level and also achieve more top grades in computers, finance and physics, traditionally male preserves.

Poor motivation and under-performance now seem to dog males all
50 through their school careers. Boys trail girls in reading and maths at every level; boys outnumber girls by two to one at schools for children with learning difficulties and 80 % of girls plan to go on to college, compared with 60 % of boys. In such statistics is hidden the shifting balance of power in the sex war.

55 The greatest challenge for men is overcoming centuries of ingrained tradition. Despite two recent recessions, working-class men still cling to the belief of a job for life and will not settle for less. Women, used to dipping in and out of the workforce to cope with family commitments, are more attuned to the new world of part-time working and short-term contracts.
60 They tend to be more adventurous and keener to extend their range of skills, even without the promise of a job.

From: Margaret Driscoll/David Thomas, *The Sunday Times*, 2 April 1995

13 *scroungers:* cf. *to scrounge:* to get (something) without work or payment or by persuading others • 34 *to store up: here:* to accumulate problems that will lead to • 44 *to outperform:* to do better than • 45 *GCSE:* General Certificate of Secondary Education

I. Questions on the text

Read all the questions first, then answer them in the given order. Use your own words as far as is appropriate.

1. Explain the crisis referred to in the first two paragraphs.

2. How does this crisis affect the angry young men's attitude to society?

3. Describe the recent changes on the job market and the consequences of these changes for both men and women.

4. Why do traditional views on the school careers of boys and girls have to be reconsidered?

5. Why, according to the writer, do women adapt more easily than men to today's job market?

6. What is the writer's attitude towards the situation of the angry young men and where does it become evident in the text?

II. Composition

Choose o n e of the following topics.

1. Our society worships the concept of youth, but cares little about young people. Discuss.

2. Staying single – a desirable way of life?

III. Translation

Translate the following text into German:

What neither sex was prepared for – according to economists, sociologists and, of course, therapists – is married women who support their husbands. As men and women play increasingly similar roles in the labor market and in marriage, the traditional exchange of housework for economic support is becoming outmoded, shifting the foundations on which many marriages are based. When traditional roles are reversed, marital problems can stack up[1] faster than dirty dishes. Men resent being turned into househusbands[2] simply because they are no longer earning big bucks. Busy professional women put in long days at the office and have less time to spend with their families. The conflicts inevitably increase the probability of divorce. Two-career couples are still trying to rewrite the rules of marriage, and in many cases both husband and wife are confused about what their roles should be. For some men, the strain of the wage disparity is tempered by their financial support of the family in the past or expectation of that responsibility in the future.

From: *Newsweek*, 15 December 1986

1 *to stack up:* to form a pile • 2 *househusband:* husband who does all the housework while his wife goes out to work

5.2. Lösungsweg und Lösungsvorschläge

I. Questions on the text

Read all the questions first, then answer them in the given order.
Use your own words as far as is appropriate.

Fragen zum Text

1. Explain the crisis referred to in the first two paragraphs.

Spezifizierung der Fragestellung

Antwort im 1. und 2. Absatz

Explain heißt hier nicht, erklärend über den Text hinauszugehen, sondern einfach nur in eigenen Worten *the crisis* zu beschreiben.
Zwar wird im 1. Textabsatz die Krise benannt, erklärt wird sie jedoch vor allem auch im 2. Textabsatz.

Stoffsammlung:

- young men regarded as not worth marrying
- women's emancipation
  → breakdown of marriage
- young unskilled men redundant
  → useless young men
- previous to this they were the backbone of industry

Formulierungsvorschlag:

The writer claims that unskilled young men are in crisis because they no longer play an important economic or social role. Years ago industry was based on young men whereas nowadays there are not enough jobs for them. Consequently today's increasingly emancipated women don't consider them suitable husbands.

2. How does this crisis affect the angry young men's attitude towards society?

Reihenfolge der Fragen spiegelt nicht Reihenfolge des Textes wider

Antwort im 3. und 6. Absatz

Nicht immer entspricht die Reihenfolge der Fragen der der Absätze, so braucht man hier Informationen aus dem 3. und 6. Textabsatz.

Stoffsammlung:

- they display antisocial behaviour, e. g. venomous football crowds, illiterate scroungers, have illegitimate children
  → further marginalisation
- they have no role in society
- they have no stable incomes, become useless partners or fathers, getting money illegitimately
  → they despise society
→ → vicious circle

Formulierungsvorschlag:

The social and economic crisis of these "angry young men" has a negative effect on their attitude towards society. The feeling of being useless causes antisocial and often aggressive behaviour such as hooliganism among these men and pushes them further towards the margin of society.

Earning no or only little money, the unskilled young men can no longer fulfil their traditional role in society as breadwinners for their families. As they are unable to find their place in society, they begin to despise it.

3. Describe the recent changes on the job market and the consequences of these changes for both men and women.

Zweiteilige Frage

Antwort im 4., 5. und 7. Absatz

Dies ist eine zweiteilige Frage, die auch in zwei Teilen beantwortet werden muss: zunächst das Nennen der *recent changes*, dann das Beschreiben der *consequences*. Auch hier ist die komplette Beantwortung der Frage nur dann möglich, wenn man sich auf mehrere Textabsätze bezieht (Absatz 4, 5 und 7).

Stoffsammlung:

changes
- more part-time working
- two out of three women now work, most of them even on a full-time basis
- traditionally male jobs will be lost
- new female jobs will be created
- there will be new jobs in service industries

consequences
- more women will be working than men
- men will no longer be the breadwinner
- women will be able to get by without men
- there will be fewer unemployed women
- men will have to swallow their contempt for "soft" jobs

Formulierungsvorschlag:

Recently there have been several changes on the job market, especially for women, because nowadays more and more women work, the majority of them even on a full-time basis. On the other hand, there is a strong trend towards part-time working. Furthermore, many jobs in once mainly male domains have been lost during the recession, whereas new jobs in the service sector have been created, especially for women.

These changes have affected the lives of both men and women considerably. Men cannot provide for families anymore. Instead, women have learned to provide for themselves. Only if men are prepared to change their attitude towards the so-called "soft jobs", i.e. jobs in the service industry, will their prospects improve.

4. Why do traditional views on the school careers of boys and girls have to be reconsidered?

Zunächst müssen die *traditional views* genannt werden, bevor die Notwendigkeit einer neuen Betrachtungsweise erläutert wird. Die Antwort auf diese Frage finden Sie in den Absätzen 8 und 9.

Zweigeteilte Fage!

Antwort im 8. und 9. Absatz

Stoffsammlung:

traditional views:
- Girls are ahead of boys until their early teens, then they fal back because of (a) the onset of puberty (b) the lower expectations of parents and teachers.

now:
- Girls outperform boys in all subjects, even in trad tionally male-dominated subjects.
- Boys are often less motivated than girls and do worse.
- They outnumber girls by two to one at schools for children with learning difficulties.
- Only 60 % of boys plan to go to college, compared with 80 % of girls.

Formulierungsvorschlag:

Traditionally, girls were thought to do better than boys at school only until the age of about ten to 13 years. Then their performance weakened because of the beginning of puberty and because teachers and parents didn't expect much of them.

The facts, however, tell a different story today. Girls do better than boys in all subjects, even in traditionally male-dominated subjects such as computers and physics, and more girls than boys intend to go to college. Moreover, boys are twice as likely as girls to develop learning cifficulties.

5. Why, according to the writer, do women adapt more easily than men to today's job market?

Hier geht es zwar um eine Meinung, aber nicht um Ihre eigene, sondern um die des Autors! Lesen Sie noch einmal den letzen Absatz durch, bevor Sie diese Frage beantworten!

Meinung des Autors ist gefragt

Antwort im letzten Absatz

Stoffsammlung:
- men: still believe in a job for life
- women: used to dipping in and out of the workforce to meet family requirements
- women: more adventurous and keener to extend their range of skills

Formulierungsvorschlag:

The writer claims that, generally speaking, women are more flexible than men. Due to their traditional role as housewives and mothers they have never been in a position to stay in one and the same full-time job throughout their whole lives. They often quit jobs when they have children and take on new jobs, frequently on a part-time basis, when the children are older. Men, however, are seldom prepared to change their job or to work part-time. Moreover, women are more willing than men to learn new skills even if they don't have a specific need for them to get a certain job.

6. What is the writer's attitude towards the situation of the angry young men and where does it become evident in the text?

Position des Autors ist gefragt

Frage nicht missverstehen!

Antwort im ganzen Text

Hier geht es darum, die Einstellung des Autors anhand konkreter Textstellen zu belegen. Gefragt ist hier nicht nach der Einschätzung der jungen Männer, sondern nach der Einschätzung ihrer Situation durch den Autor! Im Gegensatz zu den vorhergegangenen Fragen bezieht sich diese nicht auf einen oder zwei einzelne Absätze. Um sie zu beantworten, müssen Sie den gesamten Text noch einmal durchlesen, um die entsprechenden Belegstellen zu finden.

Stoffsammlung:
- "a marginalised generation … with no prospect of bettering itself" (ll. 3–4)
- "… are becoming increasingly redundant and neither employers nor women appear to have any use for them." (ll. 8–10)
- "… virtually no unskilled man can expect to play the traditional role of the breadwinner." (ll. 23–24)
- "Until men learn to be more flexible, to swallow their contempt for such 'soft' jobs, their prospects will remain grim." (ll. 39–40)
→ He sees the situation as hopeless.

Formulierungsvorschlag:

In the writer's opinion, the situation of the angry young men is bleak and hopeless. He sees them as "a marginalised generation … with no prospect of bettering itself" (ll. 3–4). Their skills no longer meet the requirements of the job market, which means that they can no longer fulfil their traditional role as the provider. So "neither employers nor women seem to have any use for them" (ll. 9–10). The writer thinks that unless men become more flexible and adjust to the changes on the job market, "their prospects will remain grim" (l. 40).

II. Comment
Choose one of the following topics.

Freie Textproduktion

Tipp
siehe S. 13

Dialektisches Thema

1. Our society worships the concept of youth, but cares little about young people. Discuss.

Formulierungsvorschlag zur Einleitung:
Whenever we switch on the TV, the commercials show happy young people enjoying the pleasures of life. This creates the impression that in today's society it is desirable to be young and that society worships the concept of youth. However, does society really care about young people?

Argumente dafür:
* Churches and sport clubs in particular offer a variety of activities for young people.
* Good education doesn't cost a fortune because primary and secondary education are free. In Germany this applies even to university.
* Most cities employ social workers and offer special programmes for marginalised young people to help them to re-integrate into society.

Argumente dagegen:
* Hardly any town offers enough attractive possibilities for young people to meet and to do things in their spare time.
* Most state schools cannot afford to employ enough teachers to provide a good education.
* The state does not support young families enough, many of them live below the poverty line.

Formulierungsvorschläge für beide Schlussvarianten:

dafür:
I am convinced that many young people who complain that society does not care enough for them are simply unwilling to see the various options society offers them – both to spend their spare time productively and to receive a decent education – in fact, all they have to do is to grasp them.

dagegen:
After weighing these arguments, I have come to the conclusion that even if there are some possibilities for young people to spend their spare time doing things, they are neither interesting nor plentiful enough to attract teenagers. This is why we cannot claim that we care enough about young people.

Tipp
siehe S. 12

Meinungsthema

2. Staying single – a desirable way of life?

Formulierungsvorschlag zur Einleitung:

Statistics show that especially the big cities are full of single households, which shows that more and more people have decided to stay single. But is this really a desirable way of life?

Argumentationshilfen dafür:

- Staying single offers independence in all major areas of life (private life, job etc).
- It is much easier to pursue a career if one does not have to show any consideration for a spouse or a family.
- In view of the high divorce rate it seems to be better to stay single.

Argumentationshilfen dagegen:

- Having a family means a certain amount of continuity in your life.
- People who don't have a family will find it difficult to learn how to take on certain responsibilities on a permanent basis.
- Singles will always have to cope with loneliness.

Formulierungsvorschläge für beide Schlussvarianten:

dafür:

I must admit that married people might find more fulfilment in life. Nevertheless it is more important for me to be independent in my choices and decisions.

dagegen:

Even though a certain amount of independence is desirable, I personally must say that the continuity of a marriage is far more important to me than being independent.

III. Translation

Das, worauf – nach Ansicht von Wirtschaftswissenschaftlern, Soziologen und natürlich Therapeuten – keines der beiden Geschlechter gefasst/vorbereitet war, sind verheiratete Frauen, die für den Lebensunterhalt ihrer Ehemänner sorgen. In dem Maße (1), in dem Männer und Frauen zunehmend ähnliche Rollen auf dem Arbeitsmarkt und in der Ehe spielen, wird der traditionelle Austausch von Hausarbeit gegen finanzielle Unterstützung (2) unzeitgemäß und verschiebt die Grundlagen, auf denen viele Ehen gegründet sind (3). Wenn traditionelle Rollen vertauscht werden, können sich Eheprobleme schneller auftürmen als schmutziges Geschirr. Männer nehmen es übel, wenn sie zu Hausmännern gemacht werden, nur weil sie nicht mehr das große Geld verdienen. Viel beschäftigte Karrierefrauen legen Überstunden im Büro ein und haben weniger Zeit, die sie mit ihren Familien verbringen. Die Konflikte erhöhen unvermeidlich/zwangsläufig die Wahrscheinlichkeit einer Scheidung. Paare, bei denen beide Ehepartner Karriere machen, versuchen noch immer, die Regeln der Ehe umzuschreiben und in vielen Fällen herrscht sowohl beim Mann als auch bei der Frau Verwirrung darüber, wie ihre Rollen aussehen sollen (4). Für einige Männer wird die Belastung, die das Auseinanderklaffen der Lohnniveaus auslöst, dadurch abgemildert, dass sie in der Vergangenheit ihre Familie finanziell versorgt haben oder durch die Erwartung, dass sie in Zukunft diese Verantwortung tragen werden.

(1) *As* am Satzanfang bedeutet zwar meist „da" oder „weil", in diesem Fall ist jedoch die zweite Bedeutung „in dem Maße" sinnvoller.

(2) „Unterstützung" allein ist hier zu wenig.

(3) *shifting the foundations* kann hier nicht mit einem beiordnenden „und" übersetzt werden, da *shifting* sich auf den ganzen vorhergehenden Satzteil bezieht.

(4) „welche Rolle sie spielen sollen" ist hier unpassend, da es nicht um die Übernahme einer Rolle, sondern um die Neudefinition der Geschlechterrolle geht.

6. A Computer ate my Book

6.1. Text und Aufgaben

By Douglas Rushkoff

Zu bearbeitender Text

Books have souls. Or so romantics like me tend to think. As I tried to reassure other book lovers last week, neither the Internet nor computers really threaten the book as an art form. As long as authors keep in mind what their books can do that no other medium can, their works will be
5 appreciated.

However, there are ways that our computerised culture is killing books. It has less to do with digital text and the Internet competing with printed media than it does with an oversimplified and, dare I say, 'mechanised' approach towards publishing and distribution.

10 Computerisation changed book publishers' system of values and cost them a lot of money in the long run. Publishers made the classic modern business mistake of trusting computers to make the decisions that should be made by humans.

The instantaneous feedback of sales records and profit margins has
15 turned the short-term 'bottom line' into a top priority. Purchased by giant media conglomerates, most book companies have had to adopt the business philosophies of their new parents: show black ink on the quarterly report. Today's ratings, calculated and analysed by computers, mean everything.

20 Such publishers no longer have time to develop new authors or invest in the "back lists" of established authors that might be valuable only over time. They have dispensed with their profitable but time-consuming 'mid-list' authors, and focused efforts on bidding for the potential blockbusters of movie stars or corrupt politicians. Publishers are investing into
25 just a few high-risk titles. When they lose, they lose big.

Computer programs also dictate the purchasing decisions of the largest retail stores, chains that now dominate the market-place. Publishers decide how many books to print based on the orders of these chains alone. These numbers are based on the previous sales records of those authors,
30 as recorded by the cash registers, reading the barcodes of books sold. The ability of an untested author to have a hit, or for an established author with low sales to get discovered by a larger audience, is greatly reduced. Grisham, Crichton and King fill the shelves, and are thus in a position to

fill the shelves again, while tomorrow's James Joyce will have to find a
35 few academics to photocopy his work. Computers, which could have
made the industry more responsive, are discouraging new growth.

This is why, although more books are being bought every year, many
publishers are actually losing money and then blaming the Internet for a
loss of interest in books. It is not the readers who have forgotten about
40 the soul of the book, it is the publishers. Computers don't kill books; people do.

Ironically, my own books about new media and cyberculture have themselves been outsmarted by computers. My first book had a cover so shiny
that no cash register's scanner could read the barcode. Sales clerks had to
45 enter the price of the book manually, often without entering the book's
computer-coded serial number. Most stores had no record of the sales of
my book and thus no automatic reordering of the text. Until the problem
was fixed, every store was out of stock yet the book had close to zero registered sales. This, in turn, translated into a lower recorded total sale of
50 books, and smaller orders the next time around.

My most recent book, 'Children of Chaos', had its title changed by my US
publisher's sales department, whose computer-analysed research had
shown that books with the word 'chaos' in the title weren't selling as well
as they once had. They renamed the book 'Playing the Future' but forgot
55 one important thing: to tell anyone. The publisher thought by simply entering the change of title into one of their own computers, that all the
bookstores and libraries would somehow implement the change, too.

None of the bookstores, not even the big chains, found out about this
new title. Their computers simply waited for the original book to show
60 up in stock. When my retitled book arrived at bookstores and ware-
houses throughout the US, most of them were promptly returned to the
publisher unopened. They hadn't ordered a book with that title! Everyone who went to a store asking for my book by its original title was told
it hadn't come in yet. Everyone who went asking for it by the new title
65 was told that it didn't exist. It wasn't in the computer, so it didn't exist in
today's book world.

Two months went by before someone figured out how to re-enter the title
of the book in the distribution computer networks, but by then it was too
late. Ordering programs dictate that if a book hasn't sold well in the first
70 three months, it shouldn't be reordered. [...]

As in any industry, computers only help when they are used by people.
The information and analysis they provide us with is extremely valuable,
but must be contextualised by real people who understand the markets

and media in which they are being employed.

75 Though I've been burned by them, I hold no grudge against the computers that ate my book or any other – just against the people who let them
do it.

(shortened)
from: *The Guardian, Online,* May 22, 1997, p. 13

I. Language/Form

1. Explain the function of the headline with regard to the stylistic device used.

2. Analyze the structure of the text.

3. Translate the following paragraph:

"… many publishers <u>are</u> actually <u>losing</u> money and then <u>blaming</u> the Internet for a loss of interest in books. It is not the readers who <u>have forgotten</u> about the soul of the book, it is the publishers. Computers <u>don't kill</u> books; people do." (lines 37–41)

4. Define the underlined verb forms (tense and aspect) and explain in English why they are used here.

II. Comprehension
Use your own words as far as possible.

1. Give three examples from the text that show the function computers have on the book market.

2. What are the effects of computerisation on the sales policies of publishers?

3. How was the author himself affected by computerisation?

IV. Comment
Choose one of the topics.

1. Computers are taking possession of people's lives. Comment on this statement.

2. Computer games: a fascinating, dangerous pastime. Discuss.

3. 'Books have souls.' (line 1)
Give a review of a work of art (book, painting, music etc.) that has really moved you.

6.2. Lösungsweg und Lösungsvorschläge

Fragen zu Sprache und Stil

Stilmittel siehe Teil C

I. Language/Form

1. Explain the function of the headline with regard to the stylistic device used.

> The stylistic device used in the headline is that of a personification. By writing that a computer ate his book, the writer implies that the computer is an animate being, as only humans or animals are capable of eating.
> The headline evokes a funny image in the reader's mind and thus makes him or her curious and eager to read on.

2. Analyze the structure of the text

> In the first two paragraphs the author states his opinion that the danger computers exert on books doesn't consist in them being an increasingly attractive medium but in producing an all too rationalistic attitude that leads to a neglection of the values many books represent.
> Paragraphs 3–7 give an outline of arguments the author uses to foster his statement.
> The following four paragraphs reflect the author's personal experiences as a writer of books.
> In the last two paragraphs the author explains his personal attitude towards computers.

3. Translate the following paragraph:

"… many publishers <u>are</u> actually <u>losing</u> money and then <u>blaming</u> the Internet for a loss of interest in books. It is not the readers who <u>have forgotten</u> about the soul of the book, it is the publishers. Computers <u>don't kill</u> books; people do." (lines 37–41)
Define the underlined verb forms (tense and aspect) and explain in English why they are used here.

> Tatsächlich verlieren viele Verleger Geld und machen dann das Internet für den Verlust des Interesses an Büchern verantwortlich. Es sind nicht die Leser, die die Seele des Buches vergessen haben, es sind die Verleger. Computer töten keine Bücher; das machen Menschen.

"are losing" and "are blaming" are both present continuous. The present continuous is used here to describe an action that is just in progress.

"have forgotten" is present perfect simple. This tense describes an action that has its beginning in the past and is still going on. The simple instead of the continuous form is used because the focus is on the action, i.e. on the forgetting itself, and not on the duration.

"don't kill": Here the present simple is not used to write about an event that is currently taking place but about a general truth.

II. Comprehension
(Use your own words as far as possible.)

1. Give three examples from the text that show the function computers have on the book market.

Sie erhalten hier mehr als die geforderten drei Beispiele aus dem gesamten Text. Suchen Sie sich diejenigen heraus, die Ihnen am wichtigsten erscheinen. Die Beispiele müssen Sie im ganzen Text suchen.

Stoffsammlung:
Computers on the book market are used to
- give instantaneous feedback of sales records and profit margins (l. 14)
- record sales figures with the help of barcode readers (ll. 29–30)
- reorder books automatically when the store runs out of stock (ll. 46–47)
- help research how well books with certain words in their title sell (ll. 52–53)
- provide us with extremely valuable information and analysis (l. 72)

Formulierungsvorschlag:
The functions that computers perform on the book market are mainly related to ordering and keeping records on sales. By means of barcode readers, computers help to keep track of the number of copies of every book sold (ll. 29–30). Moreover, they automatically order new copies, when a book runs out of stock (ll. 46–47). Finally, computers help publishers to analyse the book market. They tell shopowners how well books with certain words in their title sell (ll. 52–53).

2. What are the effects of computerisation on the sales policies of publishers?

Stoffsammlung:
- As they want to make profit as soon as possible, publishers no longer have time to take on new authors.
- Publishers prefer to search for best-selling authors rather than for quality that might pay in the long run.
- Publishers decide how many copies of a book to print on the basis of previous sales figures as recorded by the cash registers.

Formulierungsvorschlag:
Computerisation has had an enormous effect on the sales policies of publishers. Instant profit is one of the unwritten laws of the market and computers, by providing immediate results, help to make sure that sales policies are implemented accordingly: Publishers are no longer willing to invest in authors with low sales returns, even if they might prove successful in the long run. Instead, they concentrate on best-selling authors, no matter what the quality of their books is. An author's sales figures to date is the most important factor taken into account by publishers when deciding how many books to print.

3. How was the author himself affected by computerisation?

Antwort in den Absätzen 8–10

Stoffsammlung:

His first book:

- It had a cover so shiny the barcode scanner couldn't read it.
- The price had to be entered manually.
- The resulting lower sales record lead to smaller orders.

His most recent book:

- Its title contained a word which, according to computer analyses, leads to lower sales rates.
- Consequently, it had its name changed by the publisher's sales department. Book stores, however, were not informed about this change.
- When the retitled book arrived at the bookstores it was sent back.
- When anyone asked for the book by its old title, they were told it hadn't come in yet.
- When anyone asked for the book by its new title, they were told it didn't exist.
- It was not reordered because of the poor sales record.

Formulierungsvorschlag:

Scanners in bookshops were unable to read the barcode on the author's first book, so sales assistants had to enter the price manually, which, in turn, meant that hardly any sales were recorded. Thus the next order was considerably smaller than it should have been.

The title of the author's latest book was changed by his publishing house because it contained a word which, according to sales analyses, might mean lower sales rates. Retailers, however, were not automatically informed of this change. They sent back the shipment of books that bore the new title while waiting in vain for the book with the old title. So customers had no chance to buy the book. After two months the error was discovered, but then the book was not reordered because sales rates had been so poor.

III. Comment

Choose one of the topics.

1. Computers are taking possession of people's lives. Comment on this statement.

Comment on ist von der Themenstellung her mit *Discuss* gleichzusetzen. (vgl. Teil A)

Tipp
siehe S. 13

Dialektisches Thema

Formulierungsvorschlag für die Einleitung:
Sales rates for computers are ever more increasing whereas prices at the same time are falling. This indicates that there is not only a computer on practically every desktop in every office, but that people are using more and more computers in their private homes. Computers, it seems, are taking possession of people's lives.

Argumentationshilfen dafür:
- Parts of our modern world would probably break down without computers (offices, banks, travel agencies, firms etc.).
- Most private households own and use one or more computers.
- There are lots of computer and internet-addicts who, according to scientific studies, can be considered real clinical addicts.
- Thanks to modern computer technology people do not have to leave their houses any more to do the shopping or even to find friends.

Argumentationshilfen dagegen:
- People have not basically changed their work, their habits or their behaviour because of computers, the only thing that has changed is <u>the way</u> they do things.
- Many of the things people do with computers have effects on the part of their lives that has nothing to do with computers: internet acquaintances can become real friends etc.
- Many people who have to work with computers do not want to see them any more at home and prefer other spare time activities.
- There are still enough hobbies and occupations, such as sports, that do not involve computers in any way.

Formulierungsvorschlag für beide Schlussvarianten:

dafür:
Many of us do not even seem to be capable of making coffee on our own without some kind of computer. Our society has become dependant on computers to such a degree that the world comes to a standstill during a power failure. When considering all these alarming developments one cannot but be concerned about the degree to which computers are intruding people's lives. We have to be cautious and aware of the fact that computers will never be able to replace personal relationships.

dagegen:
Of course it is true that large parts of our everyday lives are very much influenced by computers. It is not true, however, that these machines are taking possession of our lives. There will always be parts of our lives that will not be dominated by computers, as every human being's need for social relationships can never be completely satisfied by machines.

2. Computer games: a fascinating, dangerous pastime. Discuss.

Tipp
siehe S. 13

Da die Themenstellung in sich schon dialektisch ist, benutzt man die beiden gegensätzlichen Adjektive als Schlagwörter für die Gliederung.

Dialektisches Thema

Formulierungsvorschlag für die Einleitung:
As the latest sales figures show, computer games are becoming more and more popular, not only with children but also with adults. While those who like playing them argue that computer games are a fascinating pastime, more and more experts warn of the dangerous effects of computer games.

Argumentationshilfen *fascinating:*
- Good computer games are a challenge to the mind and help us learn how to solve problems in a logical way.
- Computer games teach us how to concentrate.
- Computer games stimulate the imagination.
- Good computer games can be a lot of fun.

Argumentationshilfen *dangerous:*
- More and more people are overweight because they suffer from a lack of exercise due to the fact that they sit for too long in front of computers and TVs.
- Too many computer games depict violence as a legitimate means of solving conflicts.
- The danger of becoming an addict and neglecting social relationships is enormous.

Formulierungsvorschlag für beide Schlussvarianten:

fascinating:
After weighing up all the pros and cons one must admit that, even though there are computer games that affect people's minds in for the worse, they are a fascinating part of our computerized world. The human race should be intelligent enough to deal with them in a responsible way.

dangerous:
Given the fact that our world is already dominated by computers we are almost in danger of being possessed by them. It is obvious that computer games are not a healthy pastime after a day in the office or at school.

Keine verbindliche
Musterlösung möglich

3. "Books have souls." (line 1)
Give a review of a work of art (book, painting, music, etc.) that has really moved you.

Die Themenstellung ist hier zu individuell, als dass eine verbindliche Musterlösung gegeben werden könnte. Grundsätzlich sind Ihnen bei der Auswahl der Bücher, Gemälde oder Musikstücke keinerlei Grenzen gesetzt, bedenken Sie aber, dass Sie stichhaltige Argumente dafür finden müssen, warum ausgerechnet <u>dieses</u> Werk Sie besonders beeindruckt hat. Dies könnten in der Literatur Argumente aus dem Bereich der Erzählweise sein, der Personenbeschreibung oder auch des Handlungsverlaufes. Bei Musikstücken sollten Sie über fundierte musikalische Kenntnisse verfügen, um die Wirkung bestimmter Kompositionen beschreiben und beurteilen zu können. Auch im Bereich bildende Kunst sind entsprechende fachliche Kenntnisse zur Bearbeitung dieses Themas von Vorteil. Doch auch wenn Sie kein Experte auf besagten Gebieten sind, können Sie hier Punkte sammeln. Entscheidend dabei kann auch die Intensität der Beschreibung Ihrer Gefühle und Assoziationen sein.

7. Do Parents Know Their Kids?

7.1. Text und Aufgaben

Zu bearbeitender Text

Jocks, preps, punks, Goths, geeks. They may sit at separate tables in the cafeteria, but they all belong to the same generation. There are now 31 million kids in the 12-to-19 age group, and demographers predict that there will be 35 million teens by 2010. In many ways, these teens are
5 uniquely privileged. They've grown up in a period of sustained prosperity and haven't had to worry about the draft (as their fathers did) or global conflicts (as their grandparents did). Cable and the Internet have given them access to an almost infinite amount of information. Most expect to go to college, and girls, in particular, have unprecedented oppor-
10 tunities; they can dream of careers in everything from professional sports to politics, with plenty of female role models to follow.

But this positive image of American adolescence in 1999 is a little like yearbook photos that depict every kid as happy and blemish-free. After the Littleton, Colo., tragedy it's clear there's another dimension to this
15 picture, and it's far more troubled. In survey after survey, many kids say they feel increasingly alone and alienated, unable to connect with their parents, teachers and sometimes even classmates. They're desperate for guidance, and when they don't get what they need at home or in school, they cling to cliques or immerse themselves in a universe out of their par-
20 ents' reach, a world defined by computer games, TV and movies, where brutality is so common it has become mundane.

Many teens say they feel overwhelmed by pressure and responsibilities. They are juggling part-time jobs and hours of homework every night; sometimes they're so exhausted that they're nearly asleep in early-morn-
25 ing classes. Half have lived through their parents' divorce. Sixty-three percent are in households where both parents work outside the home, and many look after younger siblings in the afternoon. Still others are home by themselves after school. That unwelcome solitude can extend well into the evening; mealtime for this generation too often begins with
30 a forlorn touch of the microwave.

In fact, of all the issues that trouble adolescents, loneliness ranks at the top of the list. Teenagers may claim they want privacy, but they also crave and need attention – and they're not getting it.

Loneliness creates an emotional vacuum that is filled by an intense peer
35 culture, a critical buffer against kids' fear of isolation. Some of this bonding is normal and appropriate; in fact, studies have shown that the

human need for acceptance is almost a biological drive, like hunger. It's especially intense in early adolescence, from about 12 to 14, a time of "hyper self-consciousness," says David Elkind, a professor of child de-
40 velopment at Tufts University. "They become very self-centered and spend a lot of time thinking about what others think of them," Elkind says. "And when they think about what others are thinking, they make the error of thinking that everyone is thinking about them." Dressing alike is a refuge, a way of hiding in the group. When they're 3 and scared,
45 they cling to a security blanket; at 16, they want body piercings or Abercrombie shirts.

If parents and other adults abdicate power, teenagers come up with their own rules. Bullying has become so extreme and so common that many teens just accept it as part of high school life in the '90s. Emory University
50 psychologist Marshall Duke, an expert on children's friendships, recently asked 110 students in one of his classes if any of them had ever been threatened in high school. To his surprise, "they all raised their hand."

Even the best, most caring parents can't protect their teenagers from all problems, but involved parents can make an enormous difference. Kids
55 do listen, seize any opportunity to talk – in the car, over the breakfast table, watching TV. Parents have to work harder to get their points across. Ellen Galinsky, president of the Families and Work Institute, has studied teenagers, views of parents. "One 16-year-old told us, 'I am proud of the fact that my mother deals with me even though I try to push
60 her away. She's still there'." So pay attention now. The kids can't wait.

From: *Newsweek*, 10 May 1999

1 *jocks* (AmE infml): athletes, especially ones with few other interests • 1 *preps* (AmE infml): here: rich young people, noticeable for their expensive clothes • 1 *Goths:* young people who like Gothic music (dark metal music about death and evil) and cultivate a certain style: body piercing, black clothes and lipstick, white make-up • 1 *geeks* (AmE infml): boring people, dressed unfashionably • 6 *draft* (AmE): obligatory military service; in the 60s/70s, this meant being sent to fight in the Vietnam war • 14 t*he Littleton, Colo., tragedy:* massacre at a Colorado high school, where on April 20, 1999, two boys killed twelve fellow pupils and a teacher, injured many more, then killed themselves • 45 *security blanket:* soft blanket or toy that little children like to hold to comfort themselves • 45 *Abercrombie:* an expensive, trendy brand of clothes

I. Questions on the text

Read all the questions first, then answer them in the given order.
Use your own words as far as is appropriate.

1. In what way are today's teenagers a "uniquely privileged" (l. 5) generation?

2. Outline the various problems young people are confronted with.

3. How do adolescents react to their sense of isolation? What psychological explanations are given in the text?

4. What does the text say about the extent and the causes of bullying at American high schools?

5. What is the writer's message to parents?

6. Show that the writer uses a variety of means to make his text interesting and convincing.

II. Composition

Choose o n e of the following topics.

1. The "infinite amount of information" provided by cable TV and the Internet – a blessing or a curse?

2. Raising and teaching teens – not an easy job these days?

III. Translation

Translate the following text into German:

What is most bizarre about America's spate of school shootings is not that they have occurred, but America's reaction to them: plenty of public hand-wringing about moral decay and media violence. Inevitably, there have been further calls to beef up security at schools.
But these are all side issues, which have nothing to do with what really distinguishes America from other countries. Young people everywhere, like many of their elders, have violent fantasies. If America is in moral decline, then so is most of the rest of the world, which just as avidly consumes violent films and rock videos. Mentally disturbed people anywhere can sometimes pose a threat to others. And all schools, not just those in America, remain vulnerable to someone looking for innocent victims. But, of all rich countries, only America makes it possible for teenage misfits, the insane or anyone else determined to cause mayhem to get their hands so easily on such a terrifying array of weapons.

From: *The Economist*, 24 April 1999

7.2. Lösungsweg und Lösungsvorschläge

Fragen zum Text

I. Questions on the text
Read all the questions first, then answer them in the given order. Use your own words as for as is appropriate.

Antwort im 1. Absatz

1. In what way are today's teenagers a "uniquely privileged" (l. 5) generation?

Stoffsammlung:
- They have grown up in a period of sustained prosperity.
- They haven't had to worry about the draft or global conflicts.
- They are given access to an almost infinite amount of information.
- Most expect to go to college.
- Girls in particular have unprecedented opportunities.

Formulierungsvorschlag:
American teenagers are uniquely privileged in several respects. Firstly, they have little to worry about material well-being. Secondly, media provides them with plenty of information on anything they might be interested in. Thirdly, most of them will get the chance to receive a higher education. Furthermore, this generation need not worry about wars. Especially boys need not worry about the prospect of military action, while girls have more and better career opportunities than they have ever had before.

Antwort im 2.,3. und 4. Absatz

2. Outline the various problems young people are confronted with.

Frage nicht zu weit fassen!

Nehmen Sie hier nicht die Antwort auf die nächste Frage vorweg, in der Sie die Konsequenzen aus den *various problems* beschreiben sollen. Hier kann man bei der Beantwortung der Frage nicht chronologisch vorgehen, sondern muss zusammengehörige Punkte zusammenfassen. Die Antwort finden Sie in den Absätzen 2, 3 und 4.

Stoffsammlung:
- Kids feel increasingly alone and alienated.
- Kids feel unable to communicate with their parents, teachers and sometimes even classmates.
- Kids are desperate for guidance.
- Teens feel overwhelmed by pressure and responsibility.
- Half have lived through their parents' divorce.
- Many of them live in households where both parents work outside the homes.
- Many look after younger siblings, others are at home by themselves after school and even in the evenings.
- They crave and need attention and they are not getting it.

Formulierungsvorschlag:

Young people are confronted with various problems: As many of their parents are divorced and most of their fathers and mothers are at work all day long, teens suffer from loneliness and do not feel able to establish meaningful relationships with friends, parents and teachers. They long for attention and for someone who gives them guidance in their lives, but they find neither. Being alone at home means being responsible not only for themselves but sometimes also for their younger brothers and sisters. Apart from jobs they do to earn some pocket money, they also have to cope with homework and housework on their own.

3. How do adolescents react to their sense of isolation? What psychological explanations are given in the text?

Bei dieser zweigeteilten Frage müssen Sie zunächst darlegen, wie die Heranwachsenden auf ihre Isolation reagieren und dann zusammenfassen, welche psychologischen Erklärungen der Text dafür bereithält. Die Antwort finden Sie in den Absätzen 2 und 5.

Zweiteilige Frage

Antwort im 2. und 5. Absatz

Stoffsammlung:
Adolescents' reactions
- They cling to cliques (intense peer culture).
- They immerse themselves in a universe out of their parents' reach: computer games, TV, movies where brutality is common.

Psychological explanations
- The human need for acceptance is almost a biological drive.
- It is especially intense at the age of 12–14, a time of "hyper self-consciousness": Kids become self-centered and spend a lot of time thinking about what others think of them.

Formulierungsvorschlag:

Adolescents react to their sense of isolation in two main ways: On the one hand they look for comfort, reassurance and company in peer groups, on the other hand they withdraw from their parents' world and create their own world which is dominated by films and computer games, sometimes even violent ones.

Psychologists specialized in child development claim that this is normal to some degree, as the desire to be accepted by others is only natural. This desire is especially strong in puberty when teens are extremely self-conscious and are highly interested in their peers' opinion of them.

4. What does the text say about the extent and the causes of bullying at American high schools?

Zweiteilige Frage

Antwort im vorletzten Absatz

Auch diese Frage ist „versteckt" zweigeteilt: Sie sollen sowohl das Ausmaß als auch die Gründe der Gewalt darlegen. Die Antworten können Sie dem vorletzten Absatz entnehmen.

Stoffsammlung:

extent:
- Bullying has become so extreme and so common that many teens accept it as a part of high school life.
- Almost all students have already been threatened in high school in some way or other.

causes:
- Teenagers come up with their own rules because parents and adults abdicate power.

Formulierungsvorschlag:

For many teenagers, bullying at school has increased so much that it has become normal for them. Most of them have already experienced threatening in high school. The reason for this is quite obvious: Young people establish their own rules and laws when adults fail to provide guidance and authority.

Antwort im letzten Absatz

5. What is the writer's message to the parents?

Stoffsammlung:
- Even the most caring parents can't protect their teenagers from all problems.
- Commited parents can make an enormous difference.
- Parents should seize any opportunity to talk.
- Parents have to work harder to get their point across.
- Parents have to pay attention now because the kids can't wait.

Formulierungsvorschlag:

The writer's message to the parents is, first of all, that children cannot be shielded from all difficulties. On the other hand the writer points out that parents who care about their children do have a chance to help and influence them if they are persistent enough. The most important thing to do is to communicate with them as often as possible. The sooner they start the better it is for the kids.

6. Show that the writer uses a variety of means to make his text interesting and convincing.

Antwort im gesamten Text

Tipp
siehe S. 9

Bei solch vager Fragestellung werden im Allgemeinen nicht mehr als drei überzeugende Beispiele verlangt. Die verschiedenen Mittel müssen Sie sich im gesamten Text suchen und anhand von Zitaten belegen (vgl. Teil A).

Textstellen belegen

Stoffsammlung:
- convincing: Quotations from psychologists (professor David Elkind, l. 39; Marshall Duke, l. 50, Ellen Galinsky, l. 57, demographers, ll. 2–4), statistics (ll. 25–27)
- interesting: Enumeration of different varieties of youth culture in informal terminology at the very beginning of the article
- interesting <u>and</u> convincing: great number of vivid examples from everyday life (ll. 23–30, ll. 58–60)
- interesting <u>and</u> convincing: imperatives and short sentences in the last paragraph

Formulierungsvorschlag:
The writer uses a variety of means to make his text interesting as well as convincing. First of all, he begins his text with an enumeration of the different forms youth culture takes on by using expressions from informal youth language. Quotations from scientists such as demographers (ll. 2–4) and psychologists (ll. 39, 50, 57) make his text sound scientifically profound and thus convincing. The use of vivid examples from everyday life is one way the author manages to arouse the reader's interest and convince him of his arguments (ll. 23–30, ll. 58–60). The use of short sentences and pragmatic imperatives in the last paragraph is especially eye-catching. It makes the reader share the writer's opinion and makes him want to start doing something immediately.

II. Composition (Choose one of the following examples.)

1. The "infinite" amount of information provided by cable TV and the Internet – a blessing or a curse?

Machen Sie hier nicht den Fehler, sich auf den Segen oder Fluch des Kabelfernsehens oder des Internet im Allgemeinen zu beziehen, beschränken Sie sich vielmehr, wie in der Themenstellung verlangt, auf den Aspekt der Informationsflut.

Tipp siehe S. 13

Dialektisches Thema

Thema nicht zu weit fassen!

Formulierungsvorschlag für die Einleitung:
With the mass media and especially the Internet becoming more and more important in our lives, we are confronted with an ever-increasing amount of information. There are lots of people who are enthusiastic about this new possibility of broadening their horizons, whereas others are much more sceptical about this flood of information.

Argumentationshilfen *blessing:*
- Everyone's intellectual horizon can be broadened by the huge variety of information offered by TV and the new media.
- With a huge variety of sources of information it is possible to judge political situations and decisions in a more objective way.
- Democracy can only work when every member of a society has access to all sorts of information.

Argumentationshilfen *curse:*
- People become addicted to information, sometimes preferring to spend their spare time in front of screens to get the latest news. As a result their real lives suffer.
- Poorer members of society are disadvantaged because the lack of money denies them access to a lot of information.
- The danger of being inundated by infojunk is enormous.
- Too much information makes it difficult to pick out the really important issues.

Formulierungsvorschläge für beide Schlussvarianten:

blessing:
Undoubtedly the possibility of getting access to as much information as we want is one of the biggest achievements of the mass media age. This allows us to be fully informed about matters of importance and thus makes us independent of print media which is often biased.

curse:
The flood of information that is threatening to inundate everybody who has cable TV and the Internet is much too extensive and sometimes even confusing for anybody to be able to decide what is of real importance. As we will soon be unable to take any advantage of this infinite amount of information it will soon be of no more use to us.

2. Raising and teaching teens – not an easy job these days?

Tipp
siehe S. 12

Meinungsthema

Formulierungsvorschlag für die Einleitung:
Every now and then there have been times when universties were over-crowded with prospective teachers who considered teaching the job of their dreams. On the other hand, however, there is an increasing number of peo-ple who think that raising their own children creates enough problems these days and that it is anything but attractive to spend one's days at schools teaching teens.

Argumentationshilfen dafür:
- With an ever more demanding society bringing forth ever more deman-ding kids it has become increasingly difficult to be up to the task of tea-ching children well.
- In today's schools there are more and more children with a difficult social background (divorced and single parents, working parents who have no time for them etc.), who are accordingly difficult to teach
- The influence of the new media (TV, computer games, Internet) has often led to a loss of the ability to concentrate on one subject for any length of time.

Argumentationshilfen dagegen:
- Never before has there been so much help at hand: The media age provi-des parents as well as teachers with a huge amount of pedagogical litera-ture about education and upbringing.
- It has always been difficult to deal with children in their puberty. Their "re-bellion" has just taken on different forms.
- Teachers, parents and children share the same experience. It should the-refore not be that difficult for an open-minded adult to understand teens.

Formulierungsvorschläge für beide Schlussvarianten:

dafür:
Given the fact that nowaday's children and teens are facing many more psy-chological and social problems than they did years ago, it is obvious that teaching and raising them has become more of a challenge than it used to be.

dagegen:
Complaints about teenagers and their behaviour are as old as mankind. Every generation claims that they themselves were less difficult, more ambitious, and so on and so forth. This alone is proof enough that today's teens cannot be that terrible. Raising and teaching teens is in no way more difficult than it used to be.

III. Translation

Das, was am seltsamsten an der Flut von Schießereien an amerikanischen Schulen ist, ist nicht die Tatsache, dass sie geschehen sind, sondern die Reaktion Amerikas darauf: eine Fülle von öffentlichem Hände-über-dem-Kopf-Zusammenschlagen (1) über moralischen Verfall und Gewalt in den Medien. Zwangsläufig hat es weitere Rufe danach gegeben, die Sicherheit an Schulen zu verstärken.

Aber dies sind alles Randthemen, die nichts damit zu tun haben, was Amerika wirklich von anderen Ländern unterscheidet. Überall haben Jugendliche, ebenso wie viele ihrer Vorgänger, Gewaltfantasien. Wenn Amerika sich im moralischen Verfall befindet, dann trifft dies auch auf fast den ganzen Rest der Welt zu, der genauso begierig Gewaltfilme und Rockvideos konsumiert. Überall können geistesgestörte Menschen manchmal eine Bedrohung für andere darstellen. Und alle Schulen, nicht nur jene in Amerika, bleiben verwundbar gegenüber jemandem, der unschuldige Opfer sucht. Aber von allen reichen Ländern ermöglicht es nur Amerika jugendlichen Eigenbrötlern, Geisteskranken oder irgendjemand anderem, der dazu entschlossen ist, ein Blutbad (2) zu verursachen, so einfach an ein solch erschreckendes Aufgebot an Waffen heranzukommen.

(1) „Händeringen" passt hier nicht. Die dem englischen Ausdruck am ehesten entsprechende Geste ist hier das Hände-über-dem-Kopf-Zusammenschlagen.

(2) Die wörtlichen Übersetzungen „Chaos" oder „schwere Körperverletzung" sind hier unpassend bzw. nicht ausreichend.

Handwerkszeug

In diesem Teil werden einige wichtige Stilmittel und literarische Fachtermini genannt und erläutert sowie Ausdrücke, mithilfe derer man die Meinung des Autors wiedergeben kann, und auch Start- und Gliederungshilfen für den Einstieg und die Strukturierung Ihrer Textproduktion aufgelistet.

Die Stilmittel und literarischen Fachbegriffe werden zwar auf Deutsch erklärt, aber auf Englisch aufgelistet, da Sie in Ihrer Prüfung die englischen Begriffe verwenden müssen.

Die Formulierungshilfen sollten Sie nicht nur exemplarisch beherrschen. Bedenken Sie, dass eine möglichst abwechslungsreiche Verwendung am richtigen Platz Ihren Schreibstil erheblich verbessern und Ihnen somit auch wertvolle Punkte sichern kann.

1. Stilmittel

alliteration
Wiederholung von Anfangsbuchstaben bzw. -silben.
Meist zur Betonung und Verdeutlichung, aber auch in Zungenbrechern und um die Sprachmelodie zu unterstreichen.

z. B. *Betty bought a bit of butter …*

allusion
Anspielung, z. B. auf Personen, andere literarische Werke oder Situationen.
Vermittelt dem Leser das Gefühl der Verbundenheit mit dem Autor.

association
Das Gesagte ruft ein Bild hervor, dem es in irgendeiner Weise ähnelt.
Dient der Verdeutlichung und lässt das Gesagte plastischer erscheinen.

cliché
Ein banales, durch überstrapazierten Gebrauch abgedroschenes Stereotyp.
Dient der Verdeutlichung des Gesagten und wird oft auch in ironischer Absicht benutzt.

z. B. *hungry as a wolf*

climax
Eine Reihe graduell ansteigender Begriffe mit einem erkennbaren Höhepunkt.
Dient der Verdeutlichung und der Untermalung des Gesagten.

z. B. *He has done nothing, accomplished nothing, achieved nothing.*

comparison
siehe **metaphor** und **simile**

contrast
Gegenüberstellung von diametral entgegengesetzen Begriffen oder auch Ideen.
Dient der Unterstreichung des Gegensatzes.

z. B. *life and death*

ellipsis
Auslassung eines oder mehrerer Wörter.
Als bewusst benutztes Stilmittel führt sie zu einer kompakteren, wenn auch grammatisch inkorrekten Ausdrucksweise, kann allerdings, vor allem in der wörtlichen Rede, auf einen ungebildeten oder emotional unter Stress stehenden Sprecher hindeuten.

z. B. *Heard the news yet?*

emphasis
Betonung einzelner Wörter oder Textpassagen z. B. durch Kursivdruck, Unterstreichung, Fettdruck etc. oder auch durch Wiederholung oder ungewöhnliche Satzstellung.
Dient dazu, das Gesagte wichtiger erscheinen zu lassen als den Rest.

z. B. *It's <u>me</u> who is to blame.*

enumeration
Aufzählung von Begriffen.
Soll das Gesagte unterstreichen oder erklärt Oberbegriffe, indem untergeordnete Begriffe aufgezählt werden.

z. B. *She collected all her clothes, her trousers, T-shirts, blouses and skirts.*

euphemism
Negative Dinge werden mit einem positiveren Ausdruck bezeichnet.
Dient der Beschönigung.

z. B. *to pass away* anstatt *to die*

exaggeration
Übertreibung.
Dient der Hervorhebung, hat aber bisweilen auch einen komischen Effekt.

z. B. *I've told you about a thousand times, don't call me a loser.*

figures of speech (= imagery)
- **metaphor**
- **simile**
- **personification**
- **symbol**

generalization

Verallgemeinerung
Soll die (vermeintliche) Allgemeingültigkeit einer Aussage unterstreichen.

z. B. *All Germans drink beer.*

imagery

Bildlicher Ausdruck.
Beispiele siehe **figures of speech.**

irony

Das Gegenteil des Gemeinten wird gesagt.
Das eigentlich Gemeinte wird stärker betont, dadurch dass die Ironie ent-schlüsselt und verstanden werden muss. Außerdem kann man Zustände ver-steckt kritisieren ohne dafür belangt zu werden.

z. B. *What a clever idea!* anstatt *How stupid!*

metaphor

Indirekter Vergleich zwischen zwei Dingen oder Vorstellungen, deren oft ein-zige Gemeinsamkeit mithilfe der Metapher in den Vordergrund gerückt wird.
Vergleich ohne *as* oder *like.*
Dient dazu, das Gesagte plastischer erscheinen zu lassen und damit hervor-zuheben.

z. B. *She darted into the room*

onomatopoeia

Lautmalerei, Geräusche werden durch Wörter imitiert. Das Wort lässt an das Geräusch denken, welches es beschreibt.
Lässt das Gesagte lebendiger erscheinen.

z. B. *a buzzing fly, a hissing snake*

paradox

Aussage, die sich scheinbar selbst widerspricht, die aber eine tiefere Wahrheit beinhaltet.
Dient dazu, die darin enthaltene tiefere Wahrheit in den Vordergrund zu rücken

z. B. *I must be cruel only to be kind.* (Shakespeare, *Hamlet*)

personification

Personifizierung: Einem Ding oder Tier werden menschliche Qualitäten zuge-sprochen.
Lässt die Aussage plastischer und lebhafter erscheinen.

z. B. *The sun stared at them without mercy.*

pun

Zumeist witzig gemeintes Wortspiel, welches auf der phonetischen Ähnlichkeit oder Gleichheit von Wörtern beruht.
Lockert den Text auf humorvolle Weise auf.

z. B. *Home rule for Wales – and Moby Dick for king!*

repetition

Wiederholung von Wörtern oder Satzteilen.
Dient der Betonung und Verdeutlichung des Gesagten.

z. B. *This is a very, very difficult question.*

rhetorical question

Rhetorische Frage, auf die man eigentlich keine Antwort erwartet oder sie gar im Anschluss gleich selbst gibt.
Betont die Aussage und will die Zustimmung des Gegenübers erheischen.

z. B. *Have we come any further? – No, we have not!*

sarcasm

Sarkasmus: extreme Form der Ironie (siehe **irony**), in der bisweilen aggressiv und verletzend das Gegenteil von dem gesagt wird, was gemeint ist.
Soll provozieren.

z. B. *"I'm sure our English expert Chris will be able to give us an excellent explanation of this phenomenon."* (Angesprochen wird hier der schlechteste Schüler der Klasse.)

simile

Vergleich mit Hilfe von *as*, *like* oder *such*.
Dient der Erklärung, Veranschaulichung und Betonung.

z. B. *Love is like oxygen.*

symbol

Symbol: Etwas Abstraktes wird durch etwas Konkretes dargestellt.
Lässt das Gesagte oft geheimnisvoller oder poetischer erscheinen.

z. B. *red roses* für die Liebe

understatement

Untertreibung, macht Dinge scheinbar unwichtiger als sie tatsächlich sind.
Dient in Wirklichkeit dazu, das Gesagte hervorzuheben.

z. B. *I made two or three bucks today.* wenn man ordentlich Geld verdient hat.

2. Literarische Fachtermini und Textsorten

antagonist
Gegenspieler der Hauptfigur (siehe **protagonist, conflict**).

atmosphere
Grundstimmung eines literarischen Textes. Die Art der Beschreibung des Schauplatzes (siehe **setting**) und der Figuren (siehe **character**) bestimmt die Atmosphäre des Textes und somit auch den Eindruck des Lesers.

character
Figur: Person in einem literarischen Text.
Man unterscheidet zwischen zwei Arten von Figuren:
- **flat character:** Figur, die sich im Textverlauf nur wenig ändert und deren Charakter von nur wenigen oder sogar nur einer einzigen Eigenschaft bestimmt ist.
- **round character:** komplexe Figur, die im Textverlauf eine Entwicklung durchmacht und durch eine Vielzahl von Eigenschaften charakterisiert wird.

characterization
Beschreibung einer Figur.
Man unterscheidet zwischen zwei Arten der Charakterisierung:
- **explicit characterization:** direkte Charakterisierung durch den Erzähler, durch andere Figuren oder die zu charakterisierende Figur selbst.
- **implicit characterization:** indirekte Charakterisierung durch Handlung, Gedanken, Sprache, Verhalten, Einstellungen etc. der zu charakterisierenden Figur

climax
Höhepunkt eines literarischen Textes.

conflict
Konflikt.
Man unterscheidet zwischen zwei Arten von Konflikten:
external conflict: Konflikt zwischen zwei Figuren, meist zwischen **protagonist** und **antagonist.**
internal conflict: innerer Konflikt einer einzigen Figur, meist des **protagonist,** über gegensätzliche Werte, Wünsche etc.

drama
Ein literarisches Werk, das dazu gedacht ist, auf einer Bühne aufgeführt zu werden. Ein Drama besteht meist aus mehreren Akten, die in Szenen unterteilt sind.
Man unterscheidet zwei Hauptarten des Dramas:
- **comedy**
- **tragedy**

exposition

Einführung, die zum Thema hinführt, alle wichtigen Figuren vorstellt und den Schauplatz sowie die Atmosphäre beschreibt.

flashback

Szenen bzw. Textteile, die die Handlung unterbrechen und Begebenheiten aus der Vergangenheit wiedergeben.

mode of presentation

Art und Weise, wie eine Geschichte erzählt wird.
Man unterscheidet zwischen

- **dramatic mode of presentation:** Die Personen stellen sich selbst durch ihre Worte und Handlungen vor.
- **panoramic mode of presentation:** Der Autor stellt Handlungen während einer bestimmten Zeitspanne zusammenfassend dar. Erzählte Zeit ist länger als Erzählzeit.
- **scenic mode of presentation:** Der Autor stellt Handlungen in Einzelheiten dar. Erzählzeit kann dabei länger sein als erzählte Zeit.
- **stream of consciousness:** Der Autor stellt die inneren Bilder und Gedanken einer Figur genauso ungeordnet dar, wie sie im Kopf der Figur ablaufen.

monologue

Eine einzige Figur spricht meist über eine längere Passage hinweg. Unterarten des Monologs sind:

- **aside:** Bemerkungen oder auch kürzere Textpassagen einer Figur, die nur für das Publikum gedacht sind.
- **soliloquy:** die Figur befindet sich alleine auf der Bühne und drückt ihre Gedanken und Gefühle aus.

narrator (siehe auch **point of view**)

Erzähler, <u>nicht zu verwechseln mit dem Autor!</u>
Die Person, durch deren Augen der Leser das Geschehen sieht.
Hier unterscheidet man zwischen:

- **first person narrator:** Ich-Erzähler ist selbst Teil der Handlung und hat nur eine begrenzte Perspektive (**limited point of view**), da er nicht in die anderen Figuren hineinsehen kann.
- **third person narrator:** Erzähler, der selbst nicht Teil der Handlung ist und deshalb in der dritten Person erzählt. Er kann entweder allwissend (**omniscient narrator**) sein oder ebenfalls nur eine begrenzte Perspektive (**limited point of view**) besitzen.

novel

Roman. Längerer narrativer Text mit komplexen Strukturen, der meistens aus mehreren Kapiteln besteht.

parable

Parabel. Narrativer Text, der eine moralische Lehre vermitteln will.

playwright
Autor eines Dramas (siehe **drama**).

plot
Handlung in einer Kurzgeschichte, einem Roman oder einem Drama, die von den ihr zu Grunde liegenden Konflikten (siehe **conflict**) vorangetrieben wird. Dies führt zu einem gewissen Maß an Spannung (siehe **suspense**).

point of view
Die Perspektive, die der Erzähler (siehe **narrator**) einnimmt. Man unterscheidet vor allem zwischen
limited point of view: weil der Erzähler aus der Sicht nur einer der Figuren die Handlung beschreibt, bleibt seine Perspektive auf die dieser Person beschränkt. Solche Erzähler können entweder in der ersten (**first person narrator**) oder in der dritten Person (**third person narrator**) erzählen.
unlimited point of view: der Erzähler steht außerhalb der Handlung und hat deshalb als allwissender Erzähler (**omniscient narrator**) eine unbeschränkte Perspektive. Er erzählt immer in der dritten Person (**third person narrator**).

protagonist
Hauptfigur (siehe **antagonist, conflict**).

satire
Belehrender Text, der sich der Ironie und des Sarkasmus bedient, um der Gesellschaft ihre Verfehlungen auf humorvolle Art und Weise vorzuhalten.

setting
Zeit, Ort und soziales Umfeld der Handlung, Schauplatz.

short story
Die Kurzgeschichte ist nicht ganz klar vom Roman abzugrenzen, unterscheidet sich jedoch meist durch die folgenden Merkmale: Konzentration auf eine Figur, ein Problem oder eine Situation. Kürzer und weniger komplex als ein Roman (siehe **novel**).

suspense
Spannung in einem fiktionalen Text, ausgelöst durch Ungewissheit, Erwartung und Neugierde, was den Ausgang der Handlung (siehe **plot**) betrifft.

theme
Zentrale Idee eines literarischen Textes.

argumentative text
Textart, die dazu dient, den Leser von einer bestimmten Sache zu überzeugen. Hierzu werden in subjektiver Art und Weise Argumente vorgebracht, die den Leser dazu bringen sollen, am Ende die Meinung des Autors zu übernehmen.

choice of words
Wortwahl, die die Stilebene eines Textes ausmacht. Sie kann aus verschiedenen Registern stammen (siehe **register**).

descriptive text
Beschreibender Text, der dazu dient, dem Leser das Bild, das der Erzähler von einer Sache, einer Person oder Situation hat, zu vermitteln.

expository text
Expositorischer Text, in dem der Autor dem Leser etwas erklärt oder ihn über etwas informiert.

figurative language
Bildliche Sprache.

hard words
Wörter, die auf eine lateinische oder griechische Wurzel zurückgehen und von vielen Muttersprachlern als schwierig empfunden werden. Ihre Benutzung deutet auf eine höhere Stilebene hin (siehe **register**).

instructive text
Instruktiver Text, in dem der Autor den Leser in etwas unterweisen will, z. B. Gebrauchsanweisung.

lexical choice
Siehe **choice of words.**

narrative text
Narrativer Text, in dem dem Leser eine Handlung oder eine Reihe von Handlungen erzählt wird. Narrative Texte können sowohl fiktiv als auch nichtfiktiv sein.

register
Register. Stilebenen, die durch die Wortwahl (siehe **choice of words**) bestimmt werden, z. B. Umgangssprache (**colloquial language**), formale Sprache (**formal language**), Slang (**slang**), technische Sprache (**technical language**), faktische Sprache (**factual language**) oder informative Sprache (**informative language**).

sentence structure

Satzstruktur, die den Eindruck, den der Leser von einem Text hat, beeinflussen kann und normalerweise der Zielgruppe angepasst wird.

Hier unterscheidet man vor allem:

- **complex sentence structure:** Besteht ein Text aus komplexen Satzgefügen mit vielen Nebensätzen, so spricht er vor allem gebildetere Leser an und macht einen intellektuellen Eindruck.
- **simple sentence structure:** Ein Text mit einfacher strukturierten Sätzen, d. h. hauptsächlich einer Aneinanderreihung von Hauptsätzen, kann durch seinen Rhythmus die Argumentation vorantreiben, aber auch Ausdruck einer niedrigeren Stilebene sein.

tone

Ton des Textes, spiegelt die Einstellung des Autors dem Thema und den Lesern gegenüber wieder. Dies wird vor allem durch entsprechende Wortwahl (siehe **choice of words**) erreicht:

- critical tone
- contemptuous tone
- emotional tone
- humorous tone
- ironical tone
- sarcastic tone
- sympathetic tone

4. Formulierungshilfen

a) Ausdrücke um wiederzugeben, was der Autor sagt

Meinung des Autors wiedergeben

- to argue that
- to claim that
- to come out in favour of sth.
- to hold the opinion that
- to deny that
- to refute the idea that
- to state that
- to raise an objection
- to doubt whether
- to defend one's own view
- to base one's arguments on
- to give strong/convincing reasons for
- to provide/to give evidence
- to refer to an example
- to illustrate one's argument by
- to be certain/sure that

b) Start- und Gliederungshilfen für die Textproduktion

Einleitung

Ausdrücke, mit denen eine Einleitung beginnen kann:
- According to recent opinion polls
- Everyone knows that
- It has often been said that
- It is an indisputable fact that
- It is common knowledge that
- It is commonly believed that
- Statistics show that
- There can be no denying the fact that
- There has been a heated controversy on the question
- When watching TV or listening to the radio we frequently see/hear that

eigene Meinung

Ausdrücke zur Darstellung der eigenen Meinung
- As far as I can see
- I am convinced that
- I am of the opinion
- I believe that
- I think that
- In my opinion
- In my view
- To my mind

Ausdrücke, um Argumente miteinander zu verbinden

- *Apart from that*
- *As a consequence*
- *Besides*
- *Consequently*
- *Firstly – Secondly – Thirdly*
- *Furthermore*
- *In addition to that*
- *In the same way*
- *Likewise*
- *Moreover*
- *Similarly*
- *So*
- *Therefore*
- *Thus*
- *What is more*

Argumente verbinden

Aufzählungen

- *Firstly – Secondly – Thirdly*
- *For one thing – for another*
- *In the first place – in the second place*
- *First of all/To begin with/To start with*
- *Furthermore/Then/Besides/Moreover/In addition to that*
- *Last of all/Lastly/Finally*

Aufzählungen

Ausdrücke zur Darstellung von Gegensätzen

- *All the same*
- *Despite that*
- *Even so – even though – even if*
- *However*
- *In contrast*
- *In spite of – Despite*
- *It is true … but*
- *Nevertheless*
- *On the one hand – on the other hand*
- *Still*
- *Yet*

Gegensätze darstellen

Ausdrücke zur Verstärkung

- *And above all*
- *And what is more*
- *And what is worse*
- *It is essential*
- *It is indispensable*
- *It is of paramount importance*
- *Last but not least*
- *More important still is the fact that*

verstärkende Ausdrücke

Ausdrücke mit denen der Schluss beginnen kann

- *Comparing the advantages and disadvantages*
- *Weighing (up) all the pros and cons*
- *Taking everything into consideration/in account*
- *To say it quite bluntly*
- *On the whole*
- *To put it in a nutshell*
- *In the end*
- *Finally*
- *In short/In brief*
- *After careful consideration I have come to the conclusion that*
- *To sum up/Summing up one can say that*
- *In conclusion*

Wir möchten uns beim Bayerischen Staatsministerium für Unterricht und Kultus, beim Kultusministerium Sachsen-Anhalt und beim Oberschulamt Stuttgart für die freundliche Abdruckgenehmigung der Abituraufgaben bedanken.

Zu Death of a Salesman:
Lk Baden-Württemberg 1989: Text von Barry Gross, 1971. Text der Übersetzung aus: *Newsweek*, 7 March 1988. © 1988 Newsweek, Inc. All rights reserved. Reprinted by permission.

The Devil's Own:
Lk Sachsen-Anhalt 1998: Originaltext aus: *The Devils Own* von Christopher Newman. New York, 1997. S. 1–7. © 1997 by Columbia Pictures Industries Inc. Used by permission of Random House, Inc.

Dead Poets' Society:
Gk Sachsen-Anhalt 1996: Originaltext aus: *Dead Poets' Society* von N. H. Kleinbaum. Bantam Books, New York, 1993. S. 14–17. © 1989 by Touchstone Pictures. Used by permission of Bantam Books, a division of Random House, Inc.

Pride and Prejudice:
Lk Bayern 2000: Originaltext aus: *Pride and Prejudice* von Jane Austen, 1813. Text der Übersetzung von C. Gillie aus: Longman Companion to English Literature, ²1978.

The Birth of the Global Nation:
Lk Bayern 1993: Originaltext aus: *Time*, 20 July 1992. © 1992 Time Inc. Reprinted by permission. Text der Übersetzung aus: *Dialogue*, Vol. 6, No. 4, 1973.

Angry Young Men:
Gk Bayern 1996: Originaltext von Margaret Driscoll und David Thomas aus: *The Sunday Times*, 2 April 1995. © Times Newspaper Limited, 1995. Text der Übersetzung aus: *Newsweek*, 15 December 1986.

The Reluctant Father:
Gk Bayern 1990: Originaltext aus: *Newsweek*, 2 January 1989. Text der Übersetzung aus: J. Ryder, H. Silver *Modern English Society* 1977.

Urban Problems:
Gk Baden-Württemberg 1995: Originaltext aus: *Newsweek*, September 1991. Text der Übersetzung aus: *The Times,* 7 February 1994. © William Ress Mogg/ Times Newspaper Limited, 1994.

Mentor Abiturhilfen für die Oberstufe.
Die haben's drauf.

 ## Deutsch

Texte analysieren und interpretieren
Arbeitstechniken und Methoden (63526-3)

Wissen und Strategien fürs Abitur (63528-X)

Lektüre • Durchblick (über 40 Bände)
Deutsche Schullektüren knapp und klar erklärt:
Inhalt, Hintergrund und Interpretation

Neue Rechtschreibung (für Umsteiger)
CD-ROM (63534-4), Schautafel (63533-6)

 ## Englisch

So bestehe ich das Abitur
Lerntechniken, Arbeitsmittel,
Trainingsklausuren (63556-5)

Endspurt zum Abitur
Original-Prüfungsaufgaben mit Musterlösungen
und Lösungsweg (63557-3)

Lektüre • Durchblick (7 Bände)
Englische Schullektüren knapp und klar erklärt:
Inhalt, Hintergrund und Interpretation

 ## Latein

Übersetzen mit System (63599-9)

 ## Physik

Mechanik (63665-0)

Elektrizität und Magnetismus (63666-9)

Relativitätstheorie, Atom- und Kernphysik
(63667-7)

Physik: Mechanik (CD-ROM)
Experimentieren & Verstehen (63664-2),
ausgezeichnet mit dem digita-Preis!

Chemie

Chemie, Aufbauwissen (2 Bände)
Allgemeine u. anorganische Chemie (63680-4)
Organische Chemie (63681-2)

Mathematik

**Lineare Algebra und Analytische
Geometrie** (63650-2)

Analysis (3 Bände)
Funktionen, Grenzwerte, Stetigkeit (63645-6)
Differenzialrechnung, Exponential-
und Logarithmusfunktion (63646-4)
Integralrechnung (63647-2)

Stochastik (63649-9)

Endspurt zum Abitur
Original-Prüfungsaufgaben mit Musterlösungen und Lösungsweg (63655-3)

Biologie

Immunität, Sexualität, Blutkreislauf (63689-8)

Zellbiologie (63690-1)

Stoffwechselbiologie (63691-X)

Genetik (63692-8)

Neurobiologie (63693-6)

Verhaltensbiologie (63694-4)

Evolutionsbiologie (63695-2)

Ökologie (63696-0)

Biologica (CD-ROM, alte Rechtschreibung)
Faszination Biologie multimedial (63700-2)

(ISBN-Vorspann zur Bestellnummer: 3-580-)

**Und alles selbstverständlich in neuer Rechtschreibung.
Fragen Sie in Ihrer Buchhandlung danach!**